Revelation

Revelation

Geoffrey B. Wilson

 EVANGELICAL PRESS

EVANGELICAL PRESS
16/18 High Street, Welwyn, Herts, AL6 9EQ, England.

© Evangelical Press 1985

First published 1985

ISBN 0 85324 196 2

Cover photograph: The harbour and village of Dodekanissa, on
the Isle of Patmos. Reproduced by kind
permission of the Greece Tourist Office.

Typeset by Beaver ReproGraphics,

Printed in Great Britain by The Pitman Press, Bath.

To
Bill Barkley
of
Sao Paulo,
Brazil

Contents

	page
Preface	7
Introduction	9
Section 1: *Christ among the seven churches*	
Revelation 1	15
Revelation 2	27
Revelation 3	41
Section 2: *The Lamb and the seven seals*	
Revelation 4	53
Revelation 5	58
Revelation 6	64
Revelation 7	71
Section 3: *The seven trumpets of judgement*	
Revelation 8	77
Revelation 9	83
Revelation 10	89
Revelation 11	94
Section 4: *The woman and the dragon*	
Revelation 12	103
Revelation 13	110
Revelation 14	118
Section 5: *The seven bowls of wrath*	
Revelation 15	126
Revelation 16	130

Section 6: *The fall of Babylon*
    Revelation 17   137
    Revelation 18   145
    Revelation 19   153

Section 7: *Christ's victory over Satan*
    Revelation 20   161
    Revelation 21   168
    Revelation 22   178

Bibliography   187

Preface

Of making surveys and diagrams on Revelation there is no end, but this is an attempt to provide a brief and simple verse-by-verse commentary on the whole book. The bibliography spells out my debt to many scholars who have laboured in this difficult but rewarding field of study. I am grateful for the assistance of New College Library, Edinburgh. The commentary is based on the American Standard Version (1901), published by Thomas Nelson Inc.

GEOFFREY WILSON
Huddersfield
March 1985

THE PROVINCE OF ASIA (Western part)

Introduction

It is generally acknowledged that the last book in the Bible is the most difficult to understand, and yet its very place in the canon of Scripture underlines the vital importance of grasping the meaning of its message, for Revelation is the capstone in the edifice of divinely revealed truth. In this great unveiling of God's redemptive purpose, victory is assured to the followers of the Lamb even in the midst of their struggle with the powers of darkness, and the heavenly perspective thus granted has enabled believers in every age to stand fast against their persecutors. Hence the purpose of the book is supremely practical: it is a revelation given to promote patient endurance but not to stimulate fanciful speculation.

As to its form, Revelation (*apocalypsis*) is at once an apocalypse (1:1), a prophecy (1:3) and an epistle (1:4, 11; 22:21). Arising within Judaism after the gift of prophecy had ceased, *apocalyptic* was a type of literature in which despair associated with the present evil age encouraged reflection upon the glories of the age to come. But though Revelation draws heavily upon the symbolic imagery of apocalyptic, the differences between them are more striking than the similarities. Unlike the Jewish apocalyptists, the writer of Revelation claims the inspiration of a prophet (1:3; 22:7) and uses his own name instead of hiding his identity under some great name from the past (1:4). He does not retell history under the guise of prophecy, but teaches that the hope of future glory is firmly rooted in the historic victory of the cross (7:14). Finally, in place of the passive despair of the apocalyptists, John's faith in the power of the gospel will not allow him to abandon the present to the forces of evil, which is

why he so urgently charges his readers to 'keep the sayings of
this book'.

As a *prophetic book* Revelation is not predictive in the sense
that it is history written in advance, but it does clearly show the
working out of God's purpose in history by revealing the eternal
issues which were at stake in the crisis that confronted the
churches of the Roman province of Asia. John insists that his
book is a prophecy (1:3; 22:10, 18, 19) and, as a true forth-teller
of God's will, he delivers the word of promise and judgement to
the seven churches. Thus the key to a right understanding of the
book must be sought in the 'life situation' of those to whom it
was first addressed. In other words, he does not predict the
future in a vacuum, but relates the present to the future and so
communicates what must have been an intelligible message to
the men of his own time. It is not surprising that those who lose
sight of this fact are inclined to treat Revelation as if it were *Old
Moore's Almanac!*

It is evident from the introduction (1:4) and conclusion
(22:21) that Revelation also takes the form of *an epistle* which
was intended to be read to the seven churches (chs 2, 3) as they
met for worship (1:3; cf. Col. 4:16). Since the writer was well
known to his brethren in Asia, he introduces himself simply as
John. It is as a sharer in their tribulation (1:9) that he exhorts
them to remain faithful in the face of persecution, which threatened the church from without, and the heresies which would
undermine it from within. Most scholars agree in dating the book
towards the end of the reign of Domitian (c. A.D. 96), who was
the first emperor to persecute Christians for their refusal to join
in the worship of the imperial cult. The authority with which the
author speaks and the august nature of the revelation vouchsafed
to him both suggest that he was the apostle John, whose sojourn
in Asia was virtually proved by Isbon Beckwith after a thorough
examination of the early tradition. It has been widely claimed in
modern times that the differences between Revelation and the
fourth Gospel rule out the possibility of common authorship. But
at the end of a careful investigation H. B. Swete concluded that
the evidence 'creates a strong presumption of affinity between

the Fourth Gospel and the Apocalypse, notwithstanding their great diversity both in language and thought'.

There are three further features of Revelation which should be noted:

1. *Its numerous allusions to the Old Testament.* John's thought is so steeped in the Hebrew Scriptures that the whole book is a richly woven tapestry of Old Testament words, phrases and near quotations.

2. *Its rich treasury of hymns.* The book is filled with the songs of heaven which have constantly inspired and guided the worship of the church on earth.

3. *Its figurative language and symbolic use of numbers.* John employs strange and sometimes monstrous images to impress upon his readers the reality of the unseen spiritual contest which lies behind the persecuting power of a hostile state. Numbers are freely used to convey ideas rather than mathematical units, and the dominant place which is given to the number seven has convinced some scholars that the book consists of a series of seven parallel sections, each of which depicts the church's conflict throughout the gospel age from a different standpoint. This view was expounded by William Hendriksen in *More than Conquerors* and is also followed here.

A summary of the book of Revelation

Section 1: *Christ among the seven churches* (chs 1-3).

The seven letters speak to the church in every age, because they show that the glorified Christ is always with his people, both in judgement to call them to repentance and in grace to assure them of victory.

Section 2: *The Lamb and the seven seals* (chs 4-7).

The vision of heaven reveals the victorious Lamb as the only one who is worthy to take the book with seven seals. These he opens one by one, thus securing the judgement of the wicked and the bliss of the redeemed.

Section 3: *The seven trumpets of judgement* (chs 8-11).

The first six warning judgements fail to bring the wicked to repentance and, though the witnessing church must suffer persecution, all these wrongs are avenged when the seventh trumpet heralds the final judgement.

Section 4: *The woman and the dragon* (chs 12-14).

As the woman gives birth to a son, the dragon (Satan) waits to devour him, but the child is caught up to heaven. The dragon now persecutes the woman and is assisted by the beast from the sea and the beast from the earth. The section ends with a vision of Christ's coming in judgement.

Section 5: *The seven bowls of wrath* (chs 15, 16).

In this vision there is portrayed the outpouring of God's wrath upon the impenitent and the terror of the last judgement.

Section 6: *The fall of Babylon* (chs 17-19).

The fall of the godless city is followed by rejoicing in heaven, and the destruction of the beast and the false prophet is depicted in a further account of Christ's second coming.

Section 7: *Christ's victory over Satan* (chs 20-22).

During the gospel age Satan is bound so that he may no longer deceive the nations, but he is released for the last battle, only to be overthrown at Christ's return, when the present universe is replaced by the new heaven and the new earth.

It will be seen that the above outline identifies the so-called 'millennium' of chapter 20 with the day of salvation, and the binding of Satan during this period demonstrates Christ's *present* lordship over the powers of evil, even as it also assures the church of the success of her witness in what nevertheless remains an *evil* age.

It is hoped that the interpretation offered in this book may encourage a more sober assessment of the Apocalypse, for it is very strange that the same evangelicals who refuse to allow sceptical scholars to turn Genesis into a book of myths are still credulous enough to let Revelation become the playground for the wild fantasies of some popular writers.

Section 1

Christ among the seven churches

Revelation 1

The revelation given to John is a prophecy which is to be read to the seven churches of Asia (vv. 1-8). On Patmos John sees the glorified Christ, who instructs him to write to these churches. He describes the majestic appearance of Christ and the overwhelming effect of this vision upon him (vv. 9-20).

v. 1. The Revelation of Jesus Christ, which God gave him to show unto his servants, even the things which must shortly come to pass: and he sent and signified it by his angel unto his servant John . . .

'The Revelation of Jesus Christ' means the revelation given by him (cf. NEB). Although John is the *writer,* Jesus Christ is the real *Author* of the book. As the Mediator (5:9), Christ is the unveiler of God's purpose for his people ('his servants'), and he sent his angel (22:8, 16) to convey this transcendent mystery to John through signs and symbols ('signified'). The revelation has for its content the things which '*must* [of divine necessity] shortly come to pass'. The phrase shows that the main burden of the prophecy was intended to meet the need of John's own day by warning believers of the impending crisis of persecution, though, of course, it also speaks of more distant events (v.18). Christians may never regard history as a random and meaningless succession of events, because they know that whatever happens must serve to advance the divine plan of salvation (Rom. 8:28, 35-39).

v.2. . . . who bare witness of the word of God, and of the testimony of Jesus Christ, even of all things that he saw.

In telling all that he saw, John gave witness to the Word of God and the testimony borne by Jesus Christ. John thus describes his book as 'a revelation from God mediated by the testimony of Jesus Christ, and made known to himself in visions' (Beckwith).

v.3. Blessed is he that readeth, and they that hear the words of the prophecy, and keep the things which are written therein: for the time is at hand.

This is the first of the seven beatitudes recorded in the book (14:13; 16:15; 19:9; 20:6; 22:7, 14). Here a blessing is pronounced upon the one who reads the prophecy to the congregation and upon those who both hear and obey its message (cf. 22:7). The prophecy is not mere prediction, but a true forth-telling of the will of God for his people, who are urgently summoned to keep the words of the book because the time of their fulfilment is at hand. Thus the admonition and counsel given in the prophecy were intended to prepare the church for the hour when its faith would be tried sorely (note also v. 1).

vv. 4, 5a. John to the seven churches that are in Asia: Grace to you and peace, from him who is and who was and who is to come; and from the seven Spirits that are before his throne; and from Jesus Christ, who is the faithful witness, the firstborn of the dead, and the ruler of the kings of the earth.

'John to the seven churches that are in Asia.' Although there were other churches in Asia (e.g. Colossae, Hierapolis), the fact that John was instructed to write only to seven shows that the number is used in a symbolic sense to indicate completeness. These seven churches were selected as representative of the whole church in every age. This is evident from the repeated formula,

'He that hath an ear, let him hear what the Spirit saith to the churches,' which underlines the universal application of the message addressed to each of the churches (2:7, 11, 17, 29; 3:6, 13, 22). There is no ground for supposing that the letters to the churches are prophetic and represent successive periods of church history. R. C. Trench justly remarks on the 'arbitrary artificial character of all the attempted adaptations of Church history to these Epistles', and points out that this error results from 'a futile looking into Scripture for that which is not to be found there, — from a resolution to draw out from it that which he who draws out must first himself have put in. Men will never in this way make Scripture richer. They will have made it much poorer for themselves, if they nourish themselves out of it with the fancies of men, their own or those of others, instead of with the truths of God.'

'Grace to you and peace.' This is the distinctive Christian greeting which is found in most of the New Testament epistles. All the benefits of the gospel are summed up in the twin blessings of grace and peace. 'Grace' is the free and unmerited favour of God, and 'peace' is the state of spiritual well-being secured by that favour. The threefold source of these blessings is next set forth.

'From him who is and who was and who is to come.' In this expansion of the Greek version of Exodus 3:14, 'I am he who is', God the Father is described in terms of his eternal self-existence. As the one who eternally is, God's lordship over time embraces both the past and the future, and this truth would minister much-needed comfort at a time when the church stood under the threat of persecution. The phrase 'who is to come' is especially significant, because it foreshadows 'the general purpose of the book, which is to exhibit the comings of God in human history' (Swete). (Cf. v.7.)

'And from the seven Spirits that are before his throne.' In another instance of the symbolic use of the number seven, this image represents the Holy Spirit in the fulness of his manifold operations

in the church (3:1) and in the world (4:5; 5:6). 'The seven Spirits'
are seen 'before his throne' to show the readiness of the Holy
Spirit to accomplish the will of God. The imagery here is borrowed
from Zechariah 4, where the prophet sees a lampstand with
seven lamps ('the eyes of the Lord, which range through the whole
earth', v.10), and the meaning of the vision is 'Not by might,
nor by power, but by my Spirit, says the Lord of hosts' (v.6).

**'And from Jesus Christ, who is the faithful witness, the first-born
of the dead, and the ruler of the kings of the earth.'** This triple
title is clearly in accord with John's pastoral purpose. To encourage the fidelity of his readers, he reminds them that Jesus Christ is
1.   *'The faithful witness'*, who bore witness to the truth of God
even to the point of death (John 18:37; 1 Tim. 6:13; cf. Rev. 2:13
where the same title is given to Antipas, who also sealed his
witness with his blood);
2.   *'The first-born of the dead'*, whose unique triumph over
death has given him the rank of first-born and guaranteed the
resurrection of all who are found in him (Ps. 89:27; Col. 1:18);
3.   *'The ruler of the kings of the earth'*, who is already reigning
over Caesar, their persecutor, despite all appearances to the
contrary (cf. Eph. 1:20-22; Phil. 2:9-11; Col. 1:15-18).

vv. 5b, 6. **Unto him that loveth us, and loosed us from our sins
by his blood; and he made us to be a kingdom, to be priests unto
his God and Father; to him be the glory and the dominion for
ever and ever. Amen.**

In the first of the many doxologies of the book, praise is offered
to Jesus Christ for his abiding love and finished work of redemption. As the one who lives, he ever loves those whom he purchased
from sin's dreadful bondage at the cost of his own blood. John
next states the privileges won by the Redeemer for his people. He
collectively constituted them a 'kingdom' in which they individu-
ally serve 'his God and Father' (the expression points to a
unique relationship, cf. 2:27; 3:5, 21; 14:1) as 'priests'. It is

because believers recognize Christ as the Messiah that they are
viewed in the New Testament as the true heirs of the promises
made to Israel (Exod. 19:6; 1 Peter 2:9). First, regal dignity
belongs to the members of Christ's kingdom, for they are destined to share in his kingly rule (5:10). Secondly, each believer is
a priest. This priesthood is not limited to any order of ministry.
'All may offer the sacrifice of praise and thanksgiving: all have
direct access to the holiest through the blood of Jesus: all Christians, as priests, are to minister to one another and to plead for
one another' (Marvin Vincent). It is to Christ as the Author of
these blessings that John gratefully ascribes 'the glory and the
dominion for ever and ever. Amen'. In a salutary comment,
Trench contrasts the prominent place which is given to doxo-
logical praise in this book with the very subordinate place it
often occupies in our worship.

v.7. **Behold, he cometh with the clouds; and every eye shall see
him, and they that pierced him; and all the tribes of the earth
shall mourn over him. Even so, Amen.**

This announcement of the coming of Christ in glory to judge
the world is an adaptation of Daniel 7:13 and Zechariah 12:10.
The latter prophecy bears its original favourable sense when
applied to the first advent of Christ (John 19:37), but here the
mourning is not that of repentance but of hopeless remorse,
because the second advent will end the age of gospel opportunity
and usher in the eternal state (6:16, 17). Hence all the tribes of
the earth will then wail on account of Christ's judgement upon
them. The expression 'coming with the clouds' is best understood
as symbolizing this approaching judgement (cf. Isa. 19:1). 'Every
eye shall see him' clearly means that Christ's glorious advent will
be visible to all and hidden from none. The Bible nowhere speaks
of a 'secret' second coming. John endorses the awesome truth
thus set forth with the solemn double seal: 'Even so, Amen'.

v.8. **I am the Alpha and the Omega, saith the Lord God, who is and who was and who is to come, the Almighty.**

In Revelation it is only here and in 21:5-8 that God is introduced as the speaker. The prophecy of the previous verse is guaranteed by the one who is 'the Alpha and the Omega'. These are the first and last letters of the Greek alphabet, and the title means that as God is both the beginning and the end, the A to Z of history, nothing lies outside the scope of his sovereignty (see v.4 for comment on the second title). According to F. J. A. Hort, 'the Almighty' means 'not One who can do anything, but One who holds together and controls all things'. The title 'would thus have special force in this book as reminding the faint-hearted that in spite of all appearances of a God-forsaken world, the Ruler in the heavens was Lord over all the doings of men and controlling them all in obedience to His Supreme purposes'.

v.9. **I John, your brother and partaker with you in the tribulation and kingdom and patience which are in Jesus, was in the isle that is called Patmos, for the word of God and the testimony of Jesus.**

To express his oneness with his readers, John omits his official title and introduces himself as their 'brother' in the fellowship of suffering. It is 'in Jesus' that he shares with them 'in the tribulation and the kingdom and the patient endurance' (RSV). The order of the words is significant. As union with Jesus attracts the hostility of the world (John 16:33), so the lively assurance of a share in his kingdom enables believers patiently to endure to the end (Matt. 24:13). 'Were it not for the kingdom, which the world opposes, there would be no affliction for the partakers of the kingdom; were it not for the powers of the kingdom, its partakers could not endure' (R. C. H. Lenski). John had been banished to Patmos, a small rocky island in the Aegean Sea lying about thirty-seven miles west-southwest of Miletus, because of his preaching of 'the word of God and the testimony borne by

Jesus' (cf. v.2). Committal to an island was a device used by provincial governors to rid themselves of men of high rank whose influence upon others was deemed to be harmful.

v.10. **I was in the Spirit on the Lord's day, and I heard behind me a great voice, as of a trumpet . . .**

John's extraordinary experience on Patmos must not be confused with the normal condition of the Christian life (Rom. 8:9). 'In the Spirit' here means that John was caught up by the Spirit into a state of rapture in which he lost contact with the things of time and sense and was transported into the invisible world of spiritual realities (Ezek. 2:2; Acts 10:10; 22:7; 2 Cor. 12:1-4). This took place on the day which was known to believers as 'the Lord's day', because Christ made it pre-eminently his own when he rose from the dead and inaugurated the new age of gospel grace (John 20:1, 19; Acts 20:7; 1 Cor. 16:2). John heard behind him a voice of such penetrating power that he could only liken it to that of a trumpet, and on turning he found that it was the voice of Christ (v.12).

v.11. **. . . . saying, What thou seest, write in a book and send it to the seven churches: unto Ephesus, and unto Smyrna, and unto Pergamum, and unto Thyatira, and unto Sardis, and unto Philadelphia, and unto Laodicea.**

It is in obedience to Christ's command that John writes this book and sends it to the seven churches (see comment on v.4). As the map clearly shows (see *frontispiece*), the seven cities are mentioned in the order in which it would be natural to visit them, travelling north from Ephesus to Smyrna and Pergamum, and then inland to Thyatira, and going south to Sardis, Philadelphia and Laodicea in a rough semi-circle.

v.12. **And I turned to see the voice that spake with me. And having turned I saw seven golden candlesticks . . .**

In John's vision these churches are symbolized by seven golden 'lampstands' (ASV margin, cf. v.20). The seven-branched lamp-stand represents Israel in Zechariah 4, but here there are seven separate lampstands to emphasize the duty of each local church to reflect the light of Christ in a sin-darkened world (Matt. 5:14; Phil. 2:15, 16). It is obvious that the purpose of the lampstand is to provide light, but if it fails to fulfil this function the very reason for its existence disappears (cf. 2:5). The adjective 'golden' is frequently used in Revelation to indicate the preciousness of all that pertains to the true church of God. 'No base metal belongs in the church. In all the world there is nothing so valuable as the churches which hold aloft the shining Word of the gospel' (Lenski).

v.13. **. . . and in the midst of the candlesticks one like unto a son of man, clothed with a garment down to the foot, and girt about at the breasts with a golden girdle.**

Although now glorified, Christ is far from being remote and removed from his people, for he is seen walking in the midst of the seven lampstands (cf. 2:1). The expression 'one like unto a son of man' comes from Daniel 7:13. The word 'like' not only affirms a similarity with man, but also indicates that he is more than man and thus points to his deity.[1] As befits his divine dignity, he is arrayed in a long robe and a golden girdle (Dan. 10:5). To show that the work of redemption is complete (John 19:30), the girdle is not around the waist, as though prepared for action, but is worn high round the breast 'as by one who rests from toil in the repose of sovereignty' (W. Boyd Carpenter).

1. See E. J. Young's 'Daniel's Vision of the Son of Man' reprinted in *The Law and the Prophets*, p.443.

v.14. **And his head and his hair were white as white wool, white as snow; and his eyes were as a flame of fire . . .**

Here the white hair of 'the Ancient of days' in Daniel 7:9 is assigned to Christ to show that he shares the divine attributes of eternity and purity (cf. Isa. 1:18). The description of Christ's eyes has its source in Daniel 10:6, and it symbolizes his omniscience (Heb. 4:13). The image not only depicts 'the penetrating insight of the Son of Man; but it also expresses his indignation at the sin which his divine insight detects' (Marvin R. Vincent).

v.15. **. . . and his feet like unto burnished brass, as if it had been refined in a furnace; and his voice as the voice of many waters.**

The rare word here rendered 'burnished brass' was probably an alloy for which the metal-workers of Thyatira were famous (cf. 2:18). The appearance of Christ's feet was like this metal 'glowing in a furnace' (NIV), thus signifying the consuming fire of his approaching judgement (Dan. 10:6). His voice is compared to the deafening roar of many waters to indicate his sovereign authority over all the inhabitants of the earth (Ezek. 43:2).

v.16. **And he had in his right hand seven stars: and out of his mouth proceeded a sharp two-edged sword: and his countenance was as the sun shineth in his strength.**

In his right hand, the symbol of power and protection, Christ held seven stars, which are later identified as 'the angels of the seven churches' (see comment on v.20). Out of his mouth came a sharp two-edged sword, and this vigorous image points to the executive power of his Word, which renders any other weapon unnecessary (Isa. 11:4; 2 Thess. 2:8). For it is with this same sword that Christ purges his church (2:16) and punishes the nations (19:15). The dazzling splendour of Christ's face was like the brightness of the noonday sun. As Swete points out, this

would have reminded John of the transfiguration, 'which anticipated the glory of the ascended Christ' (Matt. 17:2).

vv.17, 18. **And when I saw him, I fell at his feet as one dead. And
he laid his right hand upon me, saying, Fear not; I am the first
and the last, and the Living one; and I was dead, and behold, I am
alive for evermore, and I have the keys of death and of Hades.**

John was so overwhelmed by the awesome majesty of Christ that
he fell at his feet as though dead, for, like the prophets before
him, he felt utterly unfit for the divine presence (Isa. 6:5; Ezek.
1:28; Dan. 8:17; 10:8, 9). Christ then laid his right hand upon
John in strengthening grace as he spoke the familiar and comfort-
ing words of reassurance: 'Fear not' (cf. Matt. 17:7).

'**I am the first and the last.**' This is an express claim to deity
(Isa. 44:6), which is well explained by Richard of St Victor (died
1173): 'First, because before me a God was not formed; last,
because after me there shall not be another. First, because all
things are from me; last, because all things are to me; from me the
beginning, to me the end. First, because I am the cause of origin;
last, because I am the judge and the end' (cited by Vincent).

'**I am the Living One; I was dead, and behold I am alive for ever
and ever!**' (NIV). As 'the Living One' Christ possesses life in
himself (John 5:26), but he is the source of life for us because he
once came under the power of death to make our doom his own
and is now alive for evermore. 'There are two wonders here: the
living One becomes dead, and the dead One is alive for evermore'
(Carpenter).

'**And I have the keys of death and of Hades.**' Having risen victorious from the grave, Christ has the keys of death and of Hades,
for he not only controls the gates of death, but also exercises
authority over the abode of departed spirits. As Christ's power
thus extends even to the unseen realm of the dead, his people

need not fear that the death threatened by their persecutors will be able to separate them from his love (Rom. 8:35-39).

v.19. **Write therefore the things which thou sawest, and the things which are, and the things which shall come to pass hereafter . . .**

Having received such an assurance of Christ's power (vv. 17, 18), John is *therefore* to write to the churches of the things he has seen. In this repetition of the command given in verse 11, the content of the book is further defined ('and', *kai*, here means *that is*) as a revelation of things present ('which are') and of things to come ('which shall come to pass hereafter'). But this does not mean that the Apocalypse can be neatly divided into two watertight compartments (e.g. present, chs 1-3; future, chs 4-22). Hence this verse does not announce the 'programme' of Revelation, except insofar as it constantly relates the present to the future. For as Beckwith points out, 'A very considerable part of the book has to do with a revelation of things existent, upon which the future is conditioned.'

v.20. **. . . the mystery of the seven stars which thou sawest in my right hand, and the seven golden candlesticks. The seven stars are the angels of the seven churches: and the seven candlesticks are seven churches.**

'As for the mystery of the seven stars which you saw in my right hand, and the seven golden lampstands, the seven stars are the angels of the seven churches and the seven lampstands are the seven churches' (RSV). In revealing the secret meaning of the stars in his right hand (v.16), Christ identifies them as the angels of the seven churches, and many equate these angels with the pastors of the churches. But it is better to understand the angels as personifying the prevailing spirit of the various churches. In the double symbolism of the stars and the lampstands there seems to be an intended contrast between the inward spiritual life of the

churches and their outward earthly embodiment. Yet these are
not separate entities, for though each letter is addressed to the
angel of the church (2:1), the concluding appeal is made directly
to the *churches* (2:7). In other words, the angel and the church
are the same under different aspects: 'The one is its spiritual
character personified; the other is the congregation of believers
who collectively possess this character' (A. Plummer).

Revelation 2

This chapter contains the first four of the letters to the seven churches of Asia. Ephesus is both faithful and discerning but has lost her first love (vv. 1-7). Smyrna is commended for remaining steadfast amid Jewish persecutions (vv. 8-11). Pergamum is still loyal despite heathen opposition, but some have fallen into moral laxity and are urged to repent (vv. 12-17). Thyatira is rebuked for permitting immorality to go unchecked, and the faithful are commanded to hold fast to what they have (vv. 18-29).

The structure of each letter follows the same general pattern:
1. A greeting: 'To the angel of the church in . . . '
2. A description of Christ, usually taken from the vision in chapter 1.
3. A commendation for faithfulness and good works (absent in the case of Laodicea).
4. A condemnation of sin (except in the case of Smyrna and Philadelphia).
5. A word of warning.
6. A call to hear: 'He that hath an ear . . . '
7. A promise to the victor.

1. The letter to the church in Ephesus (2:1-7)

Situated near the mouth of the Cayster River, Ephesus, which Pliny called 'the Light of Asia', was the largest and most important city in the province (c. 250,000 pop.). It was a key commercial centre and was famous for its devotion to the cult of Artemis (Latin, Diana), whose temple was one of the seven wonders of the ancient world (Acts 19:35). It was appropriate that the first letter should be sent to the leading church of Asia. The church in Ephesus was founded by the apostle Paul, who, on his departure after three years of ministry there, had warned its elders against false teachers (Acts 20:28-31).

v.1. **To the angel of the church in Ephesus write: These things saith he that holdeth the seven stars in his right hand, he that walketh in the midst of the seven golden candlesticks . . .**

As we have gathered from 1:20, the stars are the heavenly counterparts of the churches, while the lampstands represent their earthly existence (1:13, 16). The verse thus conveys an assurance and a warning. From a heavenly point of view, Christ firmly holds the seven stars in his right hand to show that he guarantees the salvation of his people (John 10:28). But from an earthly perspective the churches stand in need of constant correction, and so Christ is also seen walking in the midst of the lampstands to inspect their condition and administer necessary reproofs (cf. 3:19).

vv.2, 3. **I know thy works, and thy toil and patience, and that thou canst not bear evil men, and didst try them that call themselves apostles, and they are not, and didst find them false; and thou hast patience and didst bear for my name's sake, and hast not grown weary.**

'I know' indicates Christ's intimate acquaintance with the condition of the church (2:9, 13, 19; 2:1, 8, 15), for this particular word emphasizes 'the absolute clearness of mental vision which photographs all the facts of life as they pass' (Swete). The works for which the Christians in Ephesus are commended are
1.   Their intolerance of evil men and their toil in unmasking the

pretensions of these self-styled 'apostles' or itinerant 'missionaries', who are identified as the Nicolaitans in verse 6 (1 John 4:1);
2.   Their steadfast endurance for the sake of Christ's name (v.3).
'Tired in loyalty, not of it. The Ephesian church can bear anything except the presence of impostors in her membership'
(James Moffatt).

v.4. **But I have this against thee, that thou didst leave thy first love.**

Christ's charge against the church in Ephesus reveals a condition
which is fraught with danger. Despite their zeal for the truth,
their devotion had suffered a serious decline. They had lost the
fervour of their first love for Christ and for his people, the latter
being the indispensable evidence of the former (John 13:35).
Hence they are urged to repent and 'do the first works' by showing their love for Christ in self-giving love of the brethren (v.5).
Mere orthodoxy is not enough for the Searcher of all hearts, for
the greatest works are worthless without love (1 Cor. 13:1-3).

v.5. **Remember therefore whence thou art fallen, and repent, and
do the first works; or else I come to thee, and will move thy
candlestick out of its place, except thou repent.**

To correct and restore the church to the love of her espousals
(Jer. 2:2), Christ uses three striking imperatives: 'Remember . . .
repent . . . do'. They are summoned to compare the warmth of
their past devotion with the coldness of their present service, and
this humbling exercise must lead to a decisive act of repentance
resulting in the doing of the first works. It is worth noting that
the command is not, 'Feel thy first feelings,' but, 'Do the first
works.' 'The way to regain this warmth of affection is neither by
working up spasmodic emotion nor by theorizing about it, but
by doing its duties' (Moffatt). Otherwise Christ will come in swift
judgement and remove its lampstand so that it ceases to be a
church.

v.6. **But this thou hast, that thou hatest the works of the Nicolaitans, which I also hate.**

But Christ commends the Ephesian church for hating what (*not* whom) he hates, namely the *works* of the Nicolaitans. 'To share His hatred of evil is to manifest an affinity of character with Him, which is a sign of grace in Churches and in individuals' (Swete). The Nicolaitans were an early Gnostic sect, who evidently advocated sinful licence in the name of Christian liberty, on the ground that spiritual perfection could not be impaired by sensual indulgence. As Lenski points out, their founder Nicolaus is more likely to have been a disciple of Cerinthus (c. A.D. 95) than the deacon mentioned in Acts 6:5 (c. A.D. 31).

v.7. **He that hath an ear, let him hear what the Spirit saith to the churches. To him that overcometh, to him will I give to eat of the tree of life, which is in the Paradise of God.**

'He that hath an ear.' The admonition of the glorified Christ to all the churches echoes the saying he repeated so often during his earthly ministry (Matt. 11:15). His appeal to the individual stresses the need for a 'spiritual' hearing of 'spiritual' truth, for those who harden their hearts become deaf to the voice of truth (Matt. 13:15).

'Let him hear what the Spirit saith to the churches.' The words are indeed spoken by Christ, but his voice is now heard in the churches through the testimony of the Spirit as recorded in Scripture (cf. John 16:12-15).

'To him that overcometh.' This is the first of Christ's promises to the 'overcomer' in the spiritual conflict against sin. To the one who is faithful to the end, Christ will give 'to eat of the tree of life' (22:14). 'Man's exclusion from the Tree of Life (Gen. 3:22f.) is repealed by Christ on condition of a personal victory over evil. To eat of the Tree is to enjoy all that the life

of the world to come has in store for redeemed humanity'
(Swete). 'Paradise', originally a Persian word meaning 'pleasure
park', was applied to the Garden of Eden in the Greek Old
Testament (Gen. 2:8; Ezek. 28:13), and finally here denotes
heaven itself.

2. The letter to the church in Smyrna (2:8-11)

Smyrna, the only one of the seven cities still in existence (modern
Izmir), lay some thirty-five miles north of Ephesus. A beautiful
city and a prosperous port (c. 200,000 pop.), it claimed to be the
first in Asia, and as a faithful ally of Rome, was in fact the first in
the province to build a temple to the goddess Roma in 195 B.C.
Its large colony of Jews used their influence with the authorities
to persecute Christians, and they later assisted in the martyrdom
of the aged Polycarp (A.D. 156). The faithful church in Smyrna
receives the shortest letter and the warmest praise.

v.8. **And to the angel of the church in Smyrna write: These things
saith the first and the last, who was dead, and lived again . . .**

In contrast to the city which claimed to be the first of Asia in
beauty and loyalty to Rome, Christ here presents himself to his
suffering church in Smyrna as both 'the first and the last', and
therefore as the supreme controller of all that lies between (1:17).
The second title (1:18), 'who died and came to life' (RSV),
emphasizes his conquest of death to assure them that the suffering he ordains must also end in victory (vv. 10, 11).

v.9. **I know thy tribulation, and thy poverty (but thou art rich),
and the blasphemy of them that say they are Jews, and they are
not, but are a synagogue of Satan.**

Christ knows that his people in Smyrna are hard pressed and in
dire poverty because of their unflinching loyalty to him. In a

hostile environment they found it difficult to make a living, and probably pagan mobs had aggravated their plight by plundering their goods (cf. Heb. 10:34). But in contrast to the false self-estimate of the Laodicean church (3:17), Christ pronounces them rich. 'Men saw nothing there save poverty, but He who sees not as man seeth, saw the true riches which this seeming poverty concealed . . . even as He too often sees the real poverty which may lie behind the show of riches; for there are both poor rich-men and rich poor-men in his sight' (Trench). Christ also knows 'the slander' to which they are subjected by those who have forfeited the name of Jew, and are 'a synagogue of Satan' because they follow the father of lies in accusing the brethren (12:10). It is worth noticing that the three terms, 'a synagogue of Satan' (v. 9), 'Satan's throne' (v. 13) and 'the deep things of Satan' (v. 24), respectively denote Jewish, pagan and heretical antagonism to the church.

v.10. **Fear not the things which thou art about to suffer: behold, the devil is about to cast some of you into prison, that ye may be tried; and ye shall have tribulation ten days. Be thou faithful unto death, and I will give thee the crown of life.**

Christ has no word of censure for this church, but warns that worse things are in store than poverty and slander, for the devil is about to cast some of them into prison to await trial and perhaps death. They must not fear the things they are about to suffer, for though the devil's design in motivating their persecutors is destructive, the divine purpose is that, when tried, they may be found faithful. The limited time the devil is allowed for his evil work – 'ten days' indicating a short period of intense testing – shows that the whole process remains under God's control. To the one who is faithful to the end, whether he dies as a martyr or not, Christ promises the festive crown of eternal life (James 1:12). 'The Lord wants only a limited number of martyrs, but he wants all of us to be faithful unto death in whatever measure of tribulation he allots to us in order to try us' (Lenski). (Cf. Matt. 24:13).

v.11. **He that hath an ear, let him hear what the Spirit saith to the churches. He that overcometh shall not be hurt of the second death.**

'He that hath an ear . . . ' See comment on verse 7.

'He that overcometh . . . ' In a situation where faithfulness to Christ may demand the ultimate sacrifice, the 'overcomer' is assured that he shall in no way be hurt by 'the second death'. This expression is used in Revelation to designate eternal punishment (cf. 20:14, 15; 21:8). 'The essence of punishment is suffering, and suffering is consciousness. In order to be punished, the person must be conscious of a certain pain, must feel that he deserves it, and know that it is inflicted because he does . . . If God by a positive act extinguishes, at death, the remorse of a hardened villain, by extinguishing his self-consciousness, it is a strange use of language to denominate this a punishment' (W. G. T. Shedd, *The Doctrine of Endless Punishment*, p.92).

3. The letter to the church in Pergamum (2:12-17)

Pergamum, the provincial capital of Asia, was about fifty-five miles north-east of Smyrna. The city was renowned for its great buildings, its library of 200,000 volumes and its many pagan temples. The most famous of these was dedicated to Asclepius, the serpent-god of healing, and the popularity of this cult made Pergamum the 'Lourdes' of the ancient world (R. H. Charles). As the first in Asia to erect a temple to Augustus (29 B.C.), it was also the stronghold of the imperial cult, and this combination of politics and religion presented the greatest threat to Christians living in Pergamum.

v.12. **And to the angel of the church in Pergamum write: These things saith he that hath the sharp two-edged sword . . .**

It was important that those who were living under the threat of the Roman sword should be reminded that Christ wielded a far more powerful sword (1:16), with which he would visit the unfaithful in summary judgement (v. 16).

v.13. **I know where thou dwellest, even where Satan's throne is; and thou holdest fast my name, and didst not deny my faith, even in the days of Antipas my witness, my faithful one, who was killed among you, where Satan dwelleth.**

Christ knows how difficult it is to be a Christian in Pergamum where Satan dwells and has his throne. As the city was the official centre of emperor worship in Asia, any refusal to confess that 'Caesar is Lord' would be regarded as an act of disloyalty to the emperor and punishable by death. But despite the danger, the church continued to hold fast to Christ's name and had already faced one crisis without denying the faith. It was during this time of persecution that Antipas was killed. We know no more of this early martyr than is said here, but Christ's commendation of his fidelity is indeed noteworthy (cf. comment on 1:5).

v.14. **But I have a few things against thee, because thou hast there some that hold the teaching of Balaam, who taught Balak to cast a stumbling block before the children of Israel, to eat things sacrificed to idols, and to commit fornication.**

In turning from praise to censure, Christ rebukes the church for tolerating within the membership a few ('a few things' = 'some') who held to the teaching of Balaam. This false prophet appears here as the prototype of all who advocate compromise with paganism, because he taught Balak, King of Moab, how to ensnare the children of Israel by enticing them into idolatry and immorality (Num. 25:1-3; 31:16). Thus the church 'which could resist Satan in the form of the Emperor-cult was not equally proof against an insidious heresy within its own ranks' (Swete). Secure in the knowledge that the heathen gods had no real existence (1 Cor. 8:4), these 'liberated' Christians saw no harm in attending idol-feasts and embracing temple prostitutes in order to obtain pagan approval.

v.15. **So hast thou also some that hold the teaching of the Nicolaitans in like manner.**

'**So hast thou also** . . . ' The comparison suggests that the two immoral sects at Pergamum were really one and the same, for those who held to the teaching of Balaam are here identified as the Nicolaitans (v. 6). Christ thus brands the Nicolaitans as Balaamites to show his abhorrence of their vile practices (cf. v. 20).

v.16. **Repent therefore; or else I come to thee quickly, and I will make war against them with the sword of my mouth.**

The whole church is urgently summoned to repent, or else Christ will visit it in swift judgement, for, unlike vigilant Ephesus (v. 6), they had allowed this evil to go on unchecked. And just as Balaam perished by the sword (Num. 31:8), so Christ threatens to make war against his present-day followers with the sword of his mouth (cf. 19:11-15). As might be expected in a book describing the cosmic conflict with evil, there are more references to war in Revelation than in any other book in the New Testament. 'The glorified Christ is in this book a Warrior, who fights with the sharp sword of the word' (Swete).

v.17. **He that hath an ear, let him hear what the Spirit saith to the churches. To him that overcometh, to him will I give of the hidden manna, and I will give him a white stone, and upon the** stone a new name written, which no one knoweth but he that receiveth it.

'He that hath an ear . . . ' See comment on verse 7.

'To him that overcometh . . . ' The one who abstains from the forbidden idol-food will be abundantly rewarded by the gift of the hidden manna in the heavenly kingdom, for then what is now hidden will be revealed (1 John 3:2). 'The seeing of Christ as He is, and, through this beatific vision, being made like to Him, is identical with the eating of the hidden manna, which shall, as it were, be then brought forth from the sanctuary, the holy of holies of God's immediate presence, where it was withdrawn from sight so long, that all may partake of it; the glory of Christ, now shrouded and concealed, being then revealed at once to his people and in them (Col. 3:4)' (Trench). There are many explanations of what is signified by the 'white stone', but the suggestion that it is the *tessera* or token that gives admission to the heavenly banquet is the one best suited to the context ('hidden manna'). The secret name inscribed on the stone is the victor's new name, which expresses his own distinctive character. The unity of heaven does not entail loss of individuality in a vague universal oneness of being. Glorification does not eliminate the human personality but rather brings it to perfection.

4. The letter to the church in Thyatira (2:18-29)

Paradoxically the longest letter is sent to the city of least importance. Thyatira lay some forty miles south-east of Pergamum, and was notable only for its industry. Each craft had its own trade guild, and as membership involved participation in licentious pagan feasts, this naturally posed an acute problem for Christians, since it was difficult for a man to make a living without belonging to the guild of his trade (W. M. Ramsay). The daring 'solution' of the problem proposed by the self-styled prophetess 'Jezebel' accounts for the severe tone of the letter (v. 20).

v.18. **And to the angel of the church in Thyatira write: These things saith the Son of God, who hath his eyes like a flame of fire, and his feet are like unto burnished brass . . .**

Christ presents himself to this church as the divine Judge, whose flaming eyes penetrate the deceptions of the prophetess and whose brazen feet are ready to crush the enemies of truth (1:14, 15). Here the title 'the Son of God' anticipates the later allusion to Psalm 2 (vv. 26, 27).

v.19. **I know thy works, and thy love and faith and ministry and patience, and that thy last works are more than the first.**

Christ knows there is much to praise in the church of Thyatira. He approves the love shown in service, the faith manifested in patient endurance and the progress proved by the growth of good works. This advance in love and faith is in sharp contrast to the sad decline at Ephesus (v. 5). 'In Ephesus there is much zeal for orthodoxy, but little love; in Thyatira there is much love, but a carelessness about false doctrine' (Plummer).

v.20. **But I have this against thee, that thou sufferest the woman Jezebel, who calleth herself a prophetess; and she teacheth and seduceth my servants to commit fornication, and to eat things sacrificed to idols.**

The devotion of the church, though warm, was lacking in discernment and this had led to the toleration in their midst of a woman who claimed prophetic inspiration for her antinomian practices. She is here branded by Christ as 'Jezebel', because the Baal-worship introduced to Israel by that pagan queen fostered idolatry and ritual prostitution (2 Kings 9:22). Trench attributes her success to the possession of genuine spiritual powers, 'only they were such as reached her from beneath, not such as descended on her from above; for as at this time miraculous gifts of grace and power were at work in the Church, so were also their counter-feits' (cf. 1 John 4:1). By her words and shameless example (v. 22), she doubtless taught that immorality and sacrificial meals could not defile those in whom the Spirit dwells, because the gods of the trade guilds were gods in name only (1 Cor. 8:4). This doctrine was the same as that of the Nicolaitans in Pergamum (vv. 14, 15). But despite the evils found in these churches, it is significant that Christ never counsels true believers to leave in order to found a 'pure' church of their own (Harry Buis).

v.21. **And I gave her time that she should repent; and she willeth not to repent of her fornication.**

Although Christ had given the false prophetess time to repent, she continued in her determination not to change her wicked ways. 'The fact that punishment does not at once overtake sinners is constantly misunderstood by them as an evidence that it never will overtake them (Eccl. 8:11; Isa. 26:10; Ps.26:11); that God does not see, or, seeing, does not care to avenge' (Trench).

vv.22, 23a. **Behold, I cast her into a bed, and them that commit adultery with her into great tribulation, except they repent of her works. And I will kill her children with death . . .**

'Behold,' arrests attention and marks the suddenness of the judgement. Christ will turn Jezebel's bed of pleasure into a bed of suffering, and her misguided followers will share that suffering in full measure unless they repent of 'her works'. Although it may seem strange to speak of repenting of another person's works, 'the point is that those who have become partakers in her sins have abandoned their own works for hers; and it is therefore from her works that they are bidden to repent' (Plummer). But her real devotees, in contrast to those she has misled for a time, Christ will kill 'with death', which is a very emphatic way of expressing their final doom.

v.23b. . . . **and all the churches shall know that I am he that searcheth the reins and hearts: and I will give unto each one of you according to your works.**

As Jezebel and her followers were probably notorious, this terrible judgement will be a salutary object lesson for all the churches in the province. 'The reins' or kidneys were regarded as the seat of the emotions, while the term 'hearts' covers the thoughts and motives (Jer. 17:10). 'Both are subject to the scrutiny of him whose eyes are as a flame of fire (v. 18)' (Swete). Works are the sole criteria of judgement because they are the indisputable proof of character. In the Day of Judgement these works shall be seen by all as Christ sees them now, and not according to our present superficial estimates of their value (20:12; 22:12).

v.24. **But to you I say, to the rest that are in Thyatira, as many as have not this teaching, who know not the deep things of Satan, as they are wont to say; I cast upon you none other burden.**

Christ now turns to the faithful in Thyatira who do not hold this teaching, and who are willingly ignorant of 'the deep things of Satan' which the 'liberated' Jezebel and her brood claimed the right to plumb. In thus boasting of their freedom to explore Satan's domain, they would taunt timid Christians for refusing to join in the activities of the trade guilds. Presumably they argued that the immunity granted by the Spirit enabled them even to indulge in immorality without contracting defilement. 'I cast upon you none other burden' is a clear echo of Acts 15:28, and means 'I put upon you no other burden than abstinence from and protest against these abominations' (Vincent).

v.25. **Nevertheless that which ye have, hold fast till I come.**

Instead of imposing any new demands upon the faithful (v. 24),

Christ commands them once and for all to take a firm hold upon what they have been taught. 'What they have of sound doctrine, of holy living, this they must hold fast, must so grasp it that none shall wrest it from them, till the day when the Lord shall come, and bring this long and painful struggle for the maintenance of his truth to an end' (Trench).

vv.26, 27. **And he that overcometh, and he that keepeth my works unto the end, to him will I give authority over the nations: and he shall rule them with a rod of iron, as the vessels of the potter are broken to shivers; as I also have received of my Father . . .**

The overcomer is here identified as the one who keeps Christ's works to the end. 'My works' are in marked contrast to 'her works' (v. 22). 'The works are those which Christ commands, which He does, and which are the fruits of His Spirit' (Vincent). A free quotation of Psalm 2:9 shows that part of the overcomer's reward will consist of a share in Christ's rule over the nations. Having received this authority from his Father as the reward for his obedience (Phil. 2:9-11), Christ will rule as a Shepherd in the interests of his flock by smiting their enemies with a staff of iron and smashing them to pieces like pottery. As Lenski explains, the meaning of the promise is to be sought in 3:21 and 20:4. 'One by one, as we reach the end here on earth, we shall pass into heaven and there sit with Christ on his throne and together with him exercise kingly rule and authority over the nations until his Parousia.'

vv.28, 29. **. . . and I will give him the morning star. He that hath an ear, let him hear what the Spirit saith to the churches.**

Since Christ declares that he is 'the bright, the morning star' (22:16), he here promises to give himself to the overcomer. 'The conqueror is not only to share Christ's activities; he is to possess Christ' (Swete). The general exhortation is placed at the end of the last four letters, whereas in the first three it precedes the promise (for comment see v. 7).

Revelation 3

This chapter contains the last three of the letters to the seven churches of Asia. Sardis is a dead church whose few living members are bidden to awake (vv. 1-6). The faithful church of Philadelphia is promised protection in the coming hour of trial (vv. 7-13). The lukewarm church of Laodicea is summoned to repent and receive Christ who stands at the door and knocks (vv. 14-22).

5. The letter to the church in Sardis (3:1-6)

Sardis, the old capital of Lydia, was about thirty miles southeast of Thyatira. In the first century A.D. it was still famous for its woollen and dyed goods (v. 4), but its glory was long since past. The city was addicted to a life of ease and this was sadly reflected in the church. The failure to keep watch had twice led to the capture of the city, and now the church was showing the same lack of vigilance (v. 3). No external opposition or internal heresy disturbed the church, which was as peaceful as the grave.

v.1. **And to the angel of the church in Sardis write: These things saith he that hath the seven Spirits of God, and the seven stars: I know thy works, that thou hast a name that thou livest, and thou art dead.**

As the ascended Christ controls the mission of the Holy Spirit to the seven churches (see comment on 1:4, 16) the Sardians must choose whether to experience his power in quickening grace or in sudden judgement (v. 3). The phrase 'I know thy works' here introduces Christ's condemnation of the church whose reputation for life was devoid of reality. Beneath the fair façade of bustling activity, Christ saw that the church at Sardis was in fact spiritually dead.

v.2. **Be thou watchful, and establish the things that remain, which were ready to die: for I have found no works of thine perfected before my God.**

The admonition was especially appropriate to Sardis because twice in its history the acropolis had been captured through the failure of the defenders to keep watch — first by Cyrus in 549 B.C. and then by Antiochus the Great in 218 B.C. (cf. Matt. 24:42-44). Although almost past hope of recovery, a residue of spiritual life remained in the church, but prompt action was essential if the embers of devotion were to be rekindled.

'For I have not found any work of yours completed in the eyes of my God' (NEB). What would have made their deeds acceptable to God was lacking, for 'works' are 'fulfilled' only when 'they are animated by the Spirit of life' (Swete). As in John 20:17, 'my God' expresses Christ's special relationship with the Father, which is here connected with the work of judgement (cf. v. 5).

v.3. **Remember therefore how thou hast received and didst hear; and keep it, and repent. If therefore thou shalt not watch, I will come as a thief, and thou shalt not know what hour I will come upon thee.**

To stimulate a desire for recovery, Christ bids the church of Sardis to bear in mind the gospel which was entrusted to their safekeeping ('received') from the moment they came to faith ('didst hear'). They must continue to keep what they had received and, by repenting forthwith, turn from present neglect to recover their lost fervour. If this warning fails to awaken the church, Christ will come as unexpectedly as a thief and his swift judgement will take them completely by surprise (Luke 12:39). There are many preliminary visitations in judgement upon churches and individuals before the final coming in glory (2:5).

v.4. **But thou hast a few names in Sardis that did not defile their garments: and they shall walk with me in white; for they are worthy.**

But in spite of the spiritual torpor of the majority, there were a few in Sardis who had not besmirched their garments by worldly compromise. In the pagan religions 'soiled clothes disqualified the worshipper and dishonoured the god. Moral purity qualifies for spiritual communion' (Moffatt). Hence Christ promises that the undefiled minority shall walk with him in the white garments of holiness (19:8).

'For they are worthy.' 'To be accounted worthy by the Lord means to be reckoned so by his grace, the grace which gave life, developed it, kept it sound and clean to the end' (Lenski). (Cf. 1 Cor. 15:10.)

v.5. **He that overcometh shall thus be arrayed in white garments; and I will in no wise blot his name out of the book of life, and I will confess his name before my Father, and before his angels.**

Here the promise of the previous verse is repeated, but it is clear from the passive tense of the verb that the overcomer does not clothe himself, for this is the investiture of grace. The emphatic negative, 'I will in no wise blot out his name', really amounts to the strongest affirmation that the victor's name shall ever remain in the book of life. Thus the perseverance of the saints to glory confirms their foreordination in the heavenly register of the redeemed (13:8; 17:8; 21:27). Christ further promises to confess the name of the victor before his Father and his angels (Matt. 10:32; Luke 12:8). 'We may observe of this Epistle that in great part it is woven together of sayings which the Lord had already uttered in the days during which he pitched his tent among men; he is now setting his seal from heaven upon his words uttered on earth' (Trench).

v.6. **He that hath an ear, let him hear what the Spirit saith to the churches.**

See comment on 2:7.

6. The letter to the church in Philadelphia (3:7-13)

Like nearby Sardis, Philadelphia was destroyed by the great earthquake of A.D. 17. But even after it was rebuilt, many citizens were afraid to return and chose to live in the surrounding countryside. Although the city had its share of pagan cults, the letter shows that the main opposition to the church came from the synagogue. Christ has no word of blame for this church, which had remained faithful despite the active hostility of the Jews (cf. v. 9 with 2:9).

v.7. **And to the angel of the church in Philadelphia write: These things saith he that is holy, he that is true, he that hath the key of David, he that openeth and none shall shut, and that shutteth and none openeth . . .**

This needful word of reassurance is addressed to the church which upheld Christ's Messianic claims in the face of Jewish gibes. As the one who is holy and true (6:10), Christ shares the divine attributes and, as the possessor of the key of David (Isa. 22:22), he exercises supreme authority in giving or withholding admission to the new Jerusalem. Thus the Jews who claimed the power to exclude from the synagogue would find themselves shut out of the heavenly kingdom. While Christ has committed the keys of the kingdom to his church (Matt. 16:19), 'He still retains the highest administration of them in his own hands. If at any time there is error in their binding and loosing, if they make sad the heart which He has not made sad, if they speak peace to the heart to which He has not spoken peace (Ezek. 13:19), then his sentence shall stand, and not theirs' (Trench).

v.8. **I know thy works (behold, I have set before thee a door opened, which none can shut), that thou hast a little power, and didst keep my word, and didst not deny my name.**

Christ knows the works of the church in Philadelphia, for as a small company of believers they have little power, and yet they have kept his Word and not denied his name (cf. 2:13). The parenthetical promise, 'Behold, I have set before thee a door opened, which none can shut,' is taken by many in the Pauline sense of a door of missionary opportunity (1 Cor. 16:9; 2 Cor. 2:12). But in the light of the previous verse, it is more likely to be the door of the Messianic kingdom. Although the Jews boasted that the kingdom belonged to ethnic Israel, Christ assures the loyal Philadelphians that he has placed before them an open door to glory, which no one can shut.

v.9. **Behold, I give of the synagogue of Satan, of them that say they are Jews, and they are not, but do lie; behold, I will make them to come and worship before thy feet, and to know that I have loved thee.**

The repeated 'behold' marks the unexpected reversal of Jewish hopes. Those who call themselves 'the chosen of God' Christ brands 'the synagogue of Satan', for in rejecting the Messiah and persecuting his people they have shown that they are not true Jews (cf. Rom. 2:28, 29). These bitter opponents of the gospel will find out their mistake when it is too late. In the Day of Judgement Christ will make them pay homage to Gentile believers and they will know that he has loved those whom they despised. This will be the final irony for Jews who expected the Gentiles to acknowledge them (Isa. 60:14), but who will then play the rôle of the heathen in confessing that Christians are the true Israel (Charles).

v.10. Because thou didst keep the word of my patience, I also will keep thee from the hour of trial, that hour which is to come upon the whole world, to try them that dwell upon the earth.

Because the Philadelphians had kept 'the word of my endurance', Christ will keep them 'from' the hour of trial (i.e. protection from the power of Satan, rather than exemption from suffering, cf. John 17:15). 'To embrace and hold fast the gospel of the Crucified was to embrace and hold fast the Gospel of Christ's own endurance, at once as an example and as a power' (Hort). The hour of trial which was about to break upon the whole Roman world was the wave of persecution which followed the enforcement of emperor worship as a test of loyalty. The church's time of trial would test all men by bringing their true character to light, for whenever unbelievers persecute Christ's people they thereby pass judgement upon themselves.

v.11. 'I come quickly: hold fast that which thou hast, that no one take thy crown.'

It is clear from 2:16 that 'I come quickly' does not refer to Christ's final coming in glory, but to his coming to help the Philadelphians in their hour of need. He comes in every trial to succour his people and judge their persecutors. Like the faithful in Thyatira (2:25), they must hold fast to what they have, 'that no one take thy crown' (2:10). For if wicked men caused them to be unfaithful, they would forfeit this crown, and so they must always be on their guard (1 Cor. 10:12).

v.12. **He that overcometh, I will make him a pillar in the temple of my God, and he shall go out thence no more: and I will write upon him the name of my God, and the name of the city of my God, the new Jerusalem, which cometh down out of heaven from my God, and mine own new name.**

'**He that overcometh, I will make him a pillar in the sanctuary of my God, and he shall go out thence no more**' (ASV margin). This promise would have special significance for those who knew the insecurity of living in a city troubled by frequent earthquakes, which caused people to flee from the danger of falling masonry. The language is metaphorical but it conveys a great spiritual truth (21:22). 'As the pillar cannot be moved out of its place while the house stands, so a lapse from goodness will be impossible for the character which has been fixed by the final victory' (Swete).

'**And I will write upon him the name of my God.**' In view of the unsettling effect of Jewish taunts, the victor's place in glory is here trebly assured.

1. Christ will write on him the divine name to mark his possession by God. 'The struggling Christian is encouraged by hearing that a time will come when he will without any doubt become God's own, incapable of being removed or claimed by another' (Plummer).

'**And the name of the city of my God, the new Jerusalem, which cometh down out of heaven from my God.**'

2. Christ will write on him the name of the heavenly city (see comment on 21:2, 10). Even during this present life the Christian's true citizenship is in heaven (Phil. 3:20), though it is now hidden; but then 'he is openly avouched, and has a right to enter in by the gates into the city' (Trench).

'And mine own new name.'

3. Christ will write on him his own new name (19:12). This mark of ownership will initiate the victor into the mystery of Christ's full glory, which is beyond our present understanding (1 Cor. 13:12).

v.13. **He that hath an ear, let him hear what the Spirit saith to the churches.**

See comment on 2:7.

7. The letter to the church in Laodicea (3:14-22)

Prosperous Laodicea was famous for its banks, its clothing and carpets made from the local glossy black wool and its medical school, which produced a noted ear ointment and eye salve (v. 18). But for all their wealth, the Laodiceans had to drink the poor water which was piped to them from hot springs six miles away (v. 16). Although apparently flourishing, this church receives Christ's sharpest rebuke for having absorbed the complacent spirit of an affluent society. Yet the lukewarm church also receives the most cordial invitation to enjoy the tender favours of Christ's love (v. 20).

v.14. **And to the angel of the church in Laodicea write: These things saith the Amen, the faithful and true witness, the beginning of the creation of God ...**

Christ presents himself to the church, which is woefully ignorant of its real condition, as 'the Amen, the faithful and true witness' (1:5; Isa. 65:16). Since he is the divine Amen, 'in whom verity is personified' (Beckwith), he is the reliable and true witness, 'whose testimony never falls short of the truth' (Swete). As the pre-existent Son, he is also 'the beginning of the creation of God' (Col. 1:15), the uncreated source and sustainer of all things

(John 1:3; Col. 1:18; Heb. 1:3). This familiar title (cf. Col. 4:16) would remind the Laodiceans of the supreme authority and power of Christ against whose judgement there was no appeal.

v. 15. **I know thy works, that thou art neither cold nor hot: I would thou wert cold or hot.**

Christ here shatters the fatal illusion of self-sufficiency by revealing the church's true condition (v. 17). The works of the Laodiceans show that they are neither cold nor hot, but lukewarm (v. 16). They had lost their former warmth, and lapsed into a spirit of complacency which was blind to any shortcoming. There is more hope of winning the 'cold' sinner than of reheating the 'lukewarm' Christian!

'I would thou wert cold or hot.' 'The wish is not that they might grow cold rather than remain in this lukewarm state; it is more a regret that they are among those who are in a condition which is so liable to self-deception' (Carpenter).

v. 16. **So because thou art lukewarm, and neither hot nor cold, I will spew thee out of my mouth.**

A startling expression of disgust at the lukewarm religion of the Laodiceans, which was as nauseating to Christ as their own water supply was to them. This came from the hot springs at Denizli and was still tepid when it reached them. 'I will spew thee' is better rendered, 'I am about to spew thee'. It is not an irrevocable sentence of doom, but a timely word of warning which is intended to lead to their repentance (vv. 18-20).

vv. 17, 18. **Because thou sayest, I am rich, and have gotten riches, and have need of nothing; and knowest not that thou art the wretched one and miserable and poor and blind and naked:**

I counsel thee to buy of me gold refined by fire, that thou mayest become rich; and white garments, that thou mayest clothe thyself, and that the shame of thy nakedness be not made manifest; and eyesalve to anoint thine eyes, that thou mayest see.

The disease is first diagnosed (v. 17) and then the remedy prescribed (v. 18). Although rich in pride, the church was poor in grace and ignorant of its destitute condition.

'**Because thou sayest** . . . ' Evidently Laodicea's self-sufficiency in *material* things was reflected in the *spiritual* life of the church, which not only claimed to be rich but also boasted that this wealth was self-acquired. Many today cherish the same delusion that they have need of nothing when, in fact, they are spiritual paupers.

'**And knowest not** . . . ' But the true state of the church is revealed in the divine indictment: '*Thou* art the wretched one!' They had an unenviable pre-eminence in wretchedness, and this pitiable condition was due to a complete lack of the very things on which they prided themselves. 'Poor and blind and naked' shows that such confidence in their prosperity, discernment and acceptance with God was totally misplaced.

'**I counsel thee to buy of me** . . . ' Christ counsels the poverty-stricken Laodiceans to buy of *him*, and thus have all their needs supplied. This is that 'gospel-buying' which is without money and without price (Isa. 55:1). Discarding the counterfeit coinage of merit, they must trust in the gold of grace refined by Christ in the furnace of affliction, so that they may be truly rich (2 Cor. 8:9). As they could not hide their nakedness with their own black woollens, they must cover their shame with the white garments of salvation, the robe of Christ's righteousness (Isa. 61:10; cf. Toplady: 'Naked, come to thee for dress'). Finally, they must recognize that they needed more than the local eye ointment to restore their clouded vision, for only Christ could give them the anointing which would enable them to see clearly both their need and his provision for it.

v.19. **As many as I love, I reprove and chasten: be zealous therefore, and repent.**

In an abrupt change of tone, Christ assures the Laodiceans that his rebukes are the proof of his love for them. 'As many as' admits of no exceptions, for chastening is not the mark of rejection but an evidence of adoption (Prov. 3:11, 12; Heb. 12:5, 6). 'The Lord is no soft Eli to his children' (Lenski).

'**Be zealous therefore, and repent.**' Lukewarmness must be replaced by a life of continuing zeal and this dramatic change in their condition is to be marked by a decisive act of repentance.

v.20. **Behold, I stand at the door and knock: if any man hear my voice and open the door, I will come in to him, and will sup with him, and he with me.**

'Behold' is a summons to each individual to heed the promise of Christ, who condescends to stand at the heart's door and seek admittance. He not only knocks but also speaks and by his gracious words he awakens a responding love which enables the sinner to open the door and let him in. The fellowship which at once follows the sinner's reception of Christ is represented by the image of a shared meal, which was to the oriental mind a sign of the most intimate friendship. The present enjoyment of this spiritual communion anticipates the heavenly banquet, but its scope is unduly restricted by those who refer these words to the Lord's Supper.

v.21. **He that overcometh, I will give to him to sit down with me in my throne, as I also overcame, and sat down with my Father in his throne.**

This extension of the promise made to the Twelve gives every faithful disciple the same privilege of sharing in Christ's heavenly

reign (Matt. 19:28). The overcomer is pictured as enthroned
with Christ and his exaltation follows the pattern set by Christ,
who also overcame before he sat down with his Father on his
throne (2 Tim. 2:12). 'My throne' and 'his throne' are the same,
for Christ shares the Father's throne (22:1). 'This crowning
promise is made to the most unpleasing of the churches. But it
is well that thus the despondency which often succeeds the
sudden collapse of self-satisfied imaginations should be met by
so bright a prospect' (Carpenter).

v.22. **He that hath an ear, let him hear what the Spirit saith to
the churches.**

See comment on 2:7.

Section 2
The Lamb and the seven seals

Revelation 4

In this vision the door of heaven is opened to reveal God seated upon his throne (vv. 1-3). He is attended by the twenty-four elders and the four living beings who worship him as the sovereign Creator of all (vv. 4-11).

v.1. **After these things I saw, and behold, a door opened in heaven, and the first voice that I heard, a voice as of a trumpet speaking with me, one saying, Come up hither, and I will show thee the things which must come to pass hereafter.**

The change of scene from earth to heaven marks a new beginning in the book. A door in heaven is opened so that John may enter and see that God is still on the throne. It is because the destiny of the world is determined by God that his hard-pressed people on earth are assured of final victory over all their foes. The voice John hears is that of Christ (1:10), who summons him to heaven to show him what *must* (in furtherance of the divine plan, cf. 1:1) happen hereafter. For it is only from the vantage-point of heaven that earthly events can be seen in their true perspective (Rom. 8:31).

v.2. **Straightway I was in the Spirit: and behold, there was a throne set in heaven, and one sitting upon the throne . . .**

Probably John repeats his earlier statement to show that his rapture to heaven was 'in the Spirit' and not the body (cf. 1:10). His creaturely limitations were temporarily suspended to enable him to see the heavenly realities which are hidden from human gaze. 'Behold' indicates that the vision is centred upon the throne of God, which is the symbol of his divine authority and power. John does not attempt to describe the form of God, whose glory is manifested in brilliant light (v. 3; 1 Tim. 6:16), but simply says that he saw 'one sitting upon the throne'. The image depicts God as reigning from the throne and points to his continuing activity in accomplishing the divine decrees.

v.3. . . . **and he that sat was to look upon like a jasper stone and a sardius: and there was a rainbow round about the throne, like an emerald to look upon.**

According to 21:11, the jasper stone is 'clear as crystal', and it perhaps represents the dazzling brightness of God's holiness, while the blood-red sardius may stand for his avenging judgements. But a much-needed note of comfort is brought to this awesome vision by the rainbow of God's grace which surrounds the throne (Gen. 9:13). For it gives believers an impregnable assurance of their salvation 'even in and with the intimation of God's judgement on the race' (K. Rengstorf, *TDNT*, Vol. III, p.342).

v.4. **And round about the throne were four and twenty thrones: and upon the thrones I saw four and twenty elders sitting, arrayed in white garments; and on their heads crowns of gold.**

Many suppose that the twenty-four elders represent the church in its totality, but in their song of praise to the Lamb they refrain from identifying themselves with the redeemed (according to the true text of 5:9, 10), and in fact it is not until

7:9, 10 that the saints appear and ascribe their salvation to God.[1]
It is therefore more in keeping with the context to regard the
elders as angelic princes (probably belonging to the highest rank
of 'thrones', cf. Col. 1:16), who exercise priestly functions in
worshipping God and presenting the prayers of the saints (5:8)
as the heavenly counterparts of the twenty-four priestly orders
in 1 Chronicles 24:9-19. Holiness and royal dignity are symbolized by their white garments and golden crowns.

v.5. **And out of the throne proceed lightnings and voices and
thunders. And there were seven lamps of fire burning before the
throne, which are the seven Spirits of God . . .**

As in the manifestation of God's presence at Sinai (Exod. 19:16),
the lightnings and the ominous sounds ('voices') of thunder that
proceed from the throne proclaim the dreadful power and
majesty of God (cf. 8:5; 11:19; 16:18). The seven blazing torches
before the throne represent the presence of the Holy Spirit in the
plenitude of his power (see comment on 1:4).

vv.6-8. **. . . and before the throne, as it were a sea of glass like
unto crystal; and in the midst of the throne, and round about the
throne, four living creatures full of eyes before and behind. And
the first creature was like a lion, and the second creature like a
calf, and the third creature had a face as of a man, and the fourth
creature was like a flying eagle. And the four living creatures,
having each one of them six wings, are full of eyes round about
and within: and they have no rest day and night, saying, Holy,
holy, holy, is the Lord God, the Almighty, who was and who is
and who is to come.**

What John likened to 'a sea of glass' is best understood as an

1. N. B. Stonehouse, 'The Elders and Living-Beings in the Apocalypse' in *Paul before the Areopagus*, pp.88-108.

image of God's transcendence; 'it suggests the vast distance which, even in the case of one who stood at the door of heaven, intervened between himself and the Throne of God' (Swete).

'Four living-beings' (Arndt-Gingrich). The resemblance of the four living beings to the cherubim and seraphim (Isa. 6:1-3; Ezek. 1:1, 5-25; 10:20) suggests that they are the angelic throne attendants who lead the heavenly hosts in the unceasing praise of God. Their strange appearance is not intended to represent the created order before the throne, but rather depicts their characteristic qualities. They are in strength like the lion, in service like the ox, in intelligence like man and in swiftness like the eagle (so Hendriksen). With prompt obedience ('six wings') and ceaseless vigilance ('full of eyes'), they continually praise God as the thrice holy one, whose eternal being guarantees his lordship over all ages and his forthcoming triumph over the powers of evil (cf. 1:4).

vv.9-11. **And when the living creatures shall give glory and honour and thanks to him that sitteth on the throne, to him that liveth for ever and ever, the four and twenty elders shall fall down before him that sitteth on the throne, and shall worship him that liveth for ever and ever, and shall cast their crowns before the throne, saying, Worthy art thou, our Lord and our God, to receive the glory and the honour and the power: for thou didst create all things, and because of thy will they were, and were created.**

In addition to the continuous praise of the previous verse, this appears to point to the spontaneous acclamation which occurs as God manifests his sovereignty in the progressive accomplishment of redemption (cf. 5:8, 14; 11:16; 19:4). 'When' here has frequentative force and means 'as often as'. As often as the living beings give glory and honour and thanks to God, the twenty-four elders prostrate themselves before him and cast down their crowns in acknowledgement that their authority is derived from him. The sovereignty and eternity of God are stressed to show that he will rule for as long as he lives. In verse 8 the living beings praise God for his essential nature as the holy and eternal one, but the twenty-four elders celebrate the manifestation of the glory and power of God in creation. As the Creator to whom all things owe their existence, God alone is worthy of the glory, honour and power which are often usurped by finite creatures, like the Emperor Domitian, who in his madness claimed the title 'our Lord and our God'. God's will is the originating cause of all things. They existed in the mind of God ('they were') before he gave them actual existence at the appointed time ('and were created'). 'The Divine Will had made the universe a fact in the scheme of things before the Divine Power gave material expression to the fact' (Swete).

Revelation 5

God is seen holding in his right hand the seven-sealed book of the divine decrees, which only the Lamb is worthy to open, and the vision ends in a paean of praise to the victorious Lamb (vv. 1-14).

v.1. **And I saw in the right hand of him that sat on the throne a book written within and on the back, close sealed with seven seals.**

John next saw a scroll on the open palm of the one seated on the throne. The scroll was filled with writing on both sides of the papyrus, but it was sealed with seven seals to ensure the secrecy of its contents. Although the future is unknown to us, it clearly contains no surprises for God, who has already determined the destiny of the world. But the vision shows that these decrees can only be fulfilled by Christ, because he alone is the appointed executor of the divine purposes (vv. 5, 6). The scroll is never read, but as each seal is broken the drama of judgement and salvation is set forth in further symbols, which disclose only as much as God intends to reveal.

v.2. **And I saw a strong angel proclaiming with a great voice, Who is worthy to open the book, and to loose the seals thereof?**

A strong angel with a mighty voice 'is needed to be the herald of a challenge addressed to the whole creation' (Swete). He cries for someone who is 'worthy' to open the book and break its seals. The call is not for a person of superhuman strength, but for one who has the moral and spiritual fitness to fulfil God's decrees and bring history to its appointed goal. History is not a random succession of events without meaning, but it remains an enigma to those who fail to realize that Christ holds the key to the world's destiny.

v.3. **And no one in the heaven, or on the earth, or under the earth, was able to open the book, or to look thereon.**

Although the angel's challenge embraced the whole creation, no one in heaven, or on earth, or in the place of departed spirits, was able to open the book or to look inside it. This emphasis on the complete inability of any other being to open the book 'stresses the supreme worthiness of the One who is able' (Buis).

v.4. **And I wept much, because no one was found worthy to open the book, or to look thereon . . .**

John's unrestrained grief is not due to disappointment or self-pity; it expresses his distress at the apparent set-back to the divine plan for creation. As one who longs to see the accomplishment of God's purpose, he weeps because he knows that purpose will remain unfulfilled unless the scroll is opened.

v.5. **. . . and one of the elders saith unto me, Weep not; behold, the Lion that is of the tribe of Judah, the Root of David, hath overcome to open the book and the seven seals thereof.**

John's weeping is checked by one of the elders (see comment on 4:4). 'Behold' directs John's attention to the one whose conquest over sin and death gives him the right to open the seven-sealed scroll (v. 9). He is introduced by two titles which identify him as the long-promised Messiah. 'The Lion that is of the tribe of Judah' points to his royal power. The designation is derived from Genesis 49:9, 10 which promises that the sceptre shall not depart from Judah until the advent of the One to whom all sovereignty is given. 'The Root of David' alludes to Isaiah 11:1, which predicts that a new shoot will restore the rule of the house of David. As the seed of David, he entered history to become the ideal king, whose universal dominion was secured by that triumph which made all history his story.

v.6. **And I saw in the midst of the throne and of the four living creatures, and in the midst of the elders, a Lamb standing, as though it had been slain, having seven horns, and seven eyes, which are the seven Spirits of God, sent forth into all the earth.**

But instead of the victorious Lion (v. 5), John saw a Lamb which appeared to have been slain, standing in the centre of the throne, surrounded by the four living beings and the elders (3:21; 7:17). This striking paradox shows that the Lion of Judah overcame when he offered himself in lamb-like submission as the perfect sacrifice for sin (Isa. 53:7). It is through the abiding merit of his death that the risen Christ now occupies the place of highest honour in heaven (v. 9). In Revelation there are twenty-eight references to Christ as the Lamb, and this concept so dominates the rest of the book that the word virtually becomes a proper name. The seven horns symbolize the fulness of Christ's power, and the seven eyes the penetrating, creation-wide thoroughness of his vision. These all-seeing eyes are identified with 'the seven Spirits of God' (1:4) to show that the Holy Spirit is sent forth into the world by the ascended Christ (cf. John 14:26; 15:26; 16:7-11).

v.7. **And he came, and he taketh it out of the right hand of him that sat on the throne.**

The drama of the scene is vividly conveyed by the tenses of the verbs: 'And he came and has taken possession of the book from the right hand of the one upon the throne.' The Lamb's victory over sin and death proved he was worthy to take the book from the right hand of God. When Christ ascended to heaven he was invested with the authority and power to rule the world and the church in accordance with the divine decrees (Matt. 28:18; Eph. 1:20-23).

v.8. **And when he had taken the book, the four living creatures and the four and twenty elders fell down before the Lamb, having each one a harp, and golden bowls full of incense, which are the prayers of the saints.**

As soon as the Lamb had taken the book, it is reasonable to assume that he sat down with God on the throne (3:21; Heb. 1:3). Then the four living beings and the twenty-four elders acknowledged his deity as they fell down before him in worship (cf. 22:9). In accordance with their priestly function, each of the elders had a harp or lyre (a symbol of praise, cf. Ps. 33:2), and precious golden bowls full of incense, representing the accumulated prayers of God's people for the fulfilment of the divine purpose in the world (cf. 8:3-5). 'The saints are not to be thought of as present there in the court of heaven, for their prayers would not then be presented by others in their behalf' (Beckwith).

vv.9, 10. **And they sing a new song, saying, Worthy art thou to take the book, and to open the seals thereof: for thou wast slain, and didst purchase unto God with thy blood men of every tribe, and tongue, and people, and nation, and madest them to be unto our God a kingdom and priests; and they reign upon the earth.**

These celestial attendants around the throne sing a 'new' song in praise of the Lamb, whose death inaugurated the 'new' covenant and accomplished the long-awaited redemption of God's people

(Ps. 96:1; Matt. 26:28). Christ is worthy to take the book and open its seals because he was slain! He purchased for God with his blood men out of every tribe and tongue and people and nation (Acts 20:28). The universal scope of his sacrifice thus embraces men of every group to form one people. Having been made a kingdom and priests (see comment on 1:6), the redeemed already reign on earth by means of their prayers (v. 8; cf. Eph. 2:6; 1 Peter 2:9). As this is a *spiritual* reign, it must not be equated with the exercise of visible authority over their fellow-men.

'The "new song" vindicates for Jesus Christ the unique place which He has taken in the history of the world. By a supreme act of self-sacrifice He has purchased men of all races and nationalities for the service of God, founded a vast spiritual Empire, and converted human life into a priestly service and a royal dignity. He who has done this is worthy to have committed into His hands the keeping of the Book of Destiny, and to break its Seals and unroll its closely packed lengths; to preside over the whole course of events which connects His Ascension with His Return' (Swete).

vv. 11, 12. **And I saw, and I heard a voice of many angels round about the throne and the living creatures and the elders; and the number of them was ten thousand times ten thousand, and thousands of thousands; saying with a great voice, Worthy is the Lamb that hath been slain to receive the power, and riches, and wisdom, and might, and honour, and glory, and blessing.**

Next, John saw and heard an innumerable host of angels responding to this worship and praising the Lamb with a mighty shout of acclamation. Their sevenfold ascription is a complete unit governed by the definite article before the first item (*'the* power'). They acknowledge the worthiness of the Lamb who was slain to receive adoration for the qualities he possesses: his divine *power* (1 Cor. 1:24), inexhaustible *riches* (Eph. 3:8); infinite *wisdom* (Col. 2:3), executive *might* (Luke 11:22), supreme *honour* (Phil. 2:11) and eternal *glory* (John 1:14) — all of which call for the *blessing* or praise of his creatures.

v.13. **And every created thing which is in the heaven, and on the earth, and under the earth, and on the sea, and all things that are in them, heard I saying, Unto him that sitteth on the throne, and unto the Lamb, be the blessing, and the honour, and the glory, and the dominion, for ever and ever.**

John now hears all creation joining in a great fourfold doxology to God and to the Lamb, whose complete equality is acknowledged in the confession that all blessing, honour, glory and dominion belong to them for ever and ever (cf. 1:6). The adoration of creation is not a song of universal salvation, but the outcome of an assurance that God will renew his fallen world through Christ's reconciling work (Rom. 8:20-22; Col. 1:20). This linking of the Lamb with God is found throughout the book. 'Here they are linked in praise; in 6:16 they are linked in wrath; in 7:17 they are linked in ministering consolation; in 19:6, 7 they are linked in triumph. In the final vision of the book the Lord God and the Lamb are the temple (21:22) and the light (21:23), the refreshment (22:1) and sovereignty (22:3) of the celestial city' (Carpenter).

v.14. **And the four living creatures said, Amen. And the elders fell down and worshipped.**

Here the exalted spirits nearest to the throne fittingly conclude the praise they began (4:8). As the four living beings say, 'Amen' (So be it), the twenty-four elders fall down in silent worship. In the key vision of the book (chs 4, 5), John's readers are shown that the seat of sovereignty is not in Rome but in heaven and that the unfolding of God's decrees has been entrusted to their Redeemer. Persecutors cannot have the last word when God has determined to overrule even the tribulations of his people for their final good (Rom. 8:28-39).

Revelation 6

As each of the first four seals is broken, a horse and its rider appear, representing conquest, war, famine and death (vv. 1-8). The opening of the fifth seal brings to view the souls of the martyrs awaiting the day of their vindication (vv. 9-11). The dreadful calamities which follow the breaking of the sixth seal are a manifestation of the Lamb's righteous wrath (vv. 12-17).

vv.1, 2. **And I saw when the Lamb opened one of the seven seals, and I heard one of the four living creatures saying as with a voice of thunder, Come. And I saw, and behold, a white horse, and he that sat thereon had a bow; and there was given unto him a crown: and he came forth conquering, and to conquer.**

As John saw the Lamb open the first seal of the book, he heard one of the four living beings summon the first horseman with a voice of thunder. In Revelation the colours of the four horses symbolize the woes they bring: white for conquest, red for blood-shed, black for famine and pale for death (cf. Zech. 1:8-11; 6:1-8). The rider on the white horse is often identified with Christ or the progress of the gospel in the world, but the Lamb who opens the seal cannot be expected to reappear as the rider thus sent forth. In fact the only similarity between this vision and that of Christ in 19:11-16 is the colour of the horse, for the rider here holds a bow whereas Christ wields the sword of the Word. This horseman at once embarks on his career of conquest, but only because 'there was given unto him a crown' (cf. Isa. 10:5-7).

'Doubtless he thought of his own might as producing the victory. But John is sure of the sovereignty of God. The conqueror has only what God allows him to have' (Leon Morris).

vv.3, 4. **And when he opened the second seal, I heard the second living creature saying, Come. And another horse came forth, a red horse: and to him that sat thereon it was given to take peace from the earth, and that they should slay one another: and there was given unto him a great sword.**

The remaining horsemen reveal the inevitable consequences of conquest: bloodshed, famine and death! 'Victory, white-horsed and crowned, wears another aspect when viewed in the lurid light of the battlefield' (Swete). Thus John is further shown that the rider on the red horse was given the power to take peace from the earth and to cause men to slay one another. For when peace is removed the destructive instincts of men are no longer restrained. The extent of this carnage is indicated by the great sword the rider is given. War is one of the judgements of God upon an apostate race. 'The history of the world is the judgement of the world' (Friedrich von Schiller).

vv.5, 6. **And when he opened the third seal, I heard the third living creature saying, Come. And I saw, and behold, a black horse; and he that sat thereon had a balance in his hand. And I heard as it were a voice in the midst of the four living creatures saying, A measure of wheat for a shilling, and three measures of barley for a shilling; and the oil and the wine hurt thou not.**

The breaking of the third seal releases a black horse whose rider held in his hand a balance for the careful weighing of food (Ezek. 4:16). This symbol is explained by the voice John heard saying, 'A measure of wheat for a shilling (literally, a *denarius*), and three measures of barley for a shilling.' At these 'famine' prices, which were twelve times the ordinary rate, a man's daily wage would only buy enough wheat to support himself, and if he wished to provide something for his family he would have to buy barley instead. The command not to hurt the oil and the wine limits the extent of the famine. The drought is severe enough to destroy most of the cereal crops, but the deeper-rooted olive and the vine are not seriously affected.

vv. 7, 8. **And when he opened the fourth seal, I heard the voice of the fourth living creature saying, Come. And I saw, and behold, a pale horse: and he that sat upon him, his name was Death; and Hades followed with him. And there was given unto them authority over the fourth part of the earth, to kill with sword, and with famine, and with death, and by the wild beasts of the earth.**

When the fourth seal was opened there appeared a pallid horse ridden by Death and followed by Hades, for those slain by death are then delivered to the realm of the dead (cf. 1:18; 20:13, 14). This rider does not personify death in general, but is only the symbol of the deaths inflicted by the 'four sore judgements' mentioned here (cf. Ezek. 14:21). As with the severe but not catastrophic famine (v. 6), these are evidently preliminary judgements of warning, since they affect only 'the fourth part of the earth'.

The meaning of the first four seals is helpfully summarized by Swete: 'The first group of seal-openings, now completed, describes the condition of the Empire as it revealed itself to the mind of the Seer. He saw a vast world-wide power, outwardly victorious and eager for fresh conquests, yet full of the elements of unrest, danger, and misery; war, scarcity, pestilence, mortality in all its forms, abroad or ready to show themselves. This series of pictures repeats itself in history, and the militarism and lust of conquest, which it represents both in their attractive and repellent aspects, are among the forces set loose by the hand of Christ to prepare the way for His coming and the final publication of the secrets of the Sealed Book.'

vv.9, 10. And when he opened the fifth seal, I saw underneath the altar the souls of them that had been slain for the word of God, and for the testimony which they held: and they cried with a great voice, saying, How long, O Master, the holy and true, dost thou not judge and avenge our blood on them that dwell on the earth?

The opening of the fifth seal reveals the souls of the martyrs safely resting under the heavenly altar of incense, from where their impatient cry for vindication ascends to the throne of God (8:3, 4). Although they had been slain for the Word of God 'and for the witness they had borne' (RSV), John saw that they lived on in heaven, for men had no power to destroy their 'souls' (the seat and centre of that life which transcends the earthly physical existence, cf. 20:4). The martyrs address God as their 'Sovereign Lord' (NIV), and in further acknowledging him as 'the holy and true', they reinforce their plea for swift vengeance upon the wicked inhabitants of the earth who had shed their blood. They do not thirst for private revenge, but cry for public justice (Luke 18:7, 8; Rom. 12:19). For the truth they confessed will not be vindicated until the sentence of condemnation passed upon them is reversed by God's judgement of their persecutors (G. B. Caird).

v.11. And there was given them to each one a white robe; and it was said unto them, that they should rest yet for a little time, until their fellow-servants also and their brethren, who should be killed even as they were, should have fulfilled their course.

This discloses the present condition of the martyrs: 'Though they have not yet reached their final bliss, they have received the *white robe*, they are free from possibility of defilement, the victory is won, and they have *rest*' (Plummer). God's answer to their cry, 'How long?' (v. 10), is that they should rest 'for a little time' until 'the number of their fellow-servants and brothers who were to be killed as they had been, was completed' (NIV). God knows the exact number of martyrs. They are his shock troops against the powers of evil, for he has ordained that the final victory is to be won through the suffering of his chosen witnesses. The way of the cross is the way to glory (3:21). 'The vision of the martyrs under the altar shows the security of those who have already suffered, explains why God delays his final judgement, and greatly inspires John's readers to be faithful unto death and join their brethren in the company of victors' (Morris Ashcraft).

v. 12. **And I saw when he opened the sixth seal, and there was a great earthquake; and the sun became black as sackcloth of hair, and the whole moon became as blood . . .**

With the opening of the sixth seal John is given his first vision of the end. In the succeeding visions he is 'permitted to see some things more than once, but each time from a different perspective' (Lenski). Here we have a symbolic description of the physical catastrophes which will herald the end of the age. As man's revolt against his Maker is associated with his belief in the stability of the created order, the final shaking of the universe will convince the proudest rebels of their arrant folly (v. 15). The effects of this cosmic upheaval could be conveyed only by means of traditional poetic language, but those who dismiss such images as the stock phrases of Jewish apocalyptic do not thereby make the judgement they represent any less certain of fulfilment. The six signs of this day of wrath involve the complete dislocation of the universe (vv. 12-14). Of the first three, John here says that when he saw the sixth seal opened, there was a great earthquake, when the sun became as black as sackcloth and the moon as the colour of blood (cf. Joel 2:10, 31).

vv. 13, 14. **. . . and the stars of the heaven fell unto the earth, as a fig tree casteth her unripe figs when she is shaken of a great wind. And the heaven was removed as a scroll when it is rolled up; and every mountain and island were moved out of their places.**

In three further images John shows how the unleashing of God's judgement completely shatters what the ancients regarded as the fixed points of an ordered world: the stars of heaven fell to the earth like unripe figs in a violent wind; the vault of heaven was rolled up like a scroll; and on earth every mountain and island was shaken out of its place (cf. Isa. 34:4).

v.15. **And the kings of the earth, and the princes, and the chief captains, and the rich, and the strong, and every bondman and freeman, hid themselves in the caves and in the rocks of the mountains . . .**

This terrifying judgement reduces men of every class to the same condition of abject fear, as they vainly seek refuge in the caves and rocks of the mountains (Isa. 2:19). The sixfold enumeration gives special stress to the utter helplessness of those who once wielded great worldly power and influence. The kings, princes and chief captains are stripped of their authority, the rich of their security and the strong of their courage. 'Every slave and free man' covers the rest of mankind and shows that none can escape the final visitation of divine wrath.

vv.16, 17. **. . . and they say to the mountains and to the rocks, Fall on us, and hide us from the face of him that sitteth on the throne, and from the wrath of the Lamb: for the great day of their wrath is come; and who is able to stand?**

The people plead for the mountains and rocks to fall on them (Hosea 10:8), because what 'sinners dread most is not death, but the revealed Presence of God' (Swete). Now that the great day of reckoning has come, they shrink in terror from the sight of God, and 'from the wrath of the Lamb'. This paradoxical expression identifies Christ as the agent of divine judgement, for those who spurn his sacrifice must endure his wrath. As the phrase 'their wrath' indicates, the Lamb's wrath is the manifestation of the wrath of God upon a sinful world. There is nothing impersonal about God's wrath; it is the necessary response of his holiness to persistent wickedness (F. F. Bruce). Since the question, 'Who is able to stand?' assumes that nobody can do so, John next describes the preservation of the righteous 'and their raptured praises, a joyous contrast with the despairing fate of those whose doom has just been narrated' (Plummer).

Revelation 7

In contrast to the doom of the wicked, John next sees the sealing of the 144,000, who represent the true Israel of God in all its fulness (vv. 1-8). This pledge of security is followed by the vision of its realization in heaven, where the 144,000 are seen to be an innumerable host, who have triumphed over tribulation and entered into the state of final blessedness (vv. 9-17).

v.1. **After this I saw four angels standing at the four corners of the earth, holding the four winds of the earth, that no wind should blow on the earth, or on the sea, or upon any tree.**

'After this' does not indicate chronological sequence, but simply introduces the vision which answers the solemn question of the last chapter: 'Who is able to stand?' As the four winds are another symbol for the four horsemen (cf. the explicit identification in Zech. 6:5), the first scene of this vision shows that the sealing of God's people is effected *before* the judgements of 6:1-8 can take place (vv. 1-8). John saw four angels holding back the winds of judgement which were ready to blow from every quarter, for 'those tempests would not arise or shake a single leaf till the securing of God's servants was accomplished' (Carpenter).

vv.2, 3. **And I saw another angel ascend from the sunrising, having the seal of the living God: and he cried with a great voice to the four angels, to whom it was given to hurt the earth and the sea,** saying, Hurt not the earth, neither the sea, nor the trees, till we shall have sealed the servants of our God on their foreheads.

The approach of another angel from the east ('sunrising') is appropriate, as God's gracious manifestations were expected from that direction (Ezek. 43:2; Mal. 4:2). The angel's task is to impress 'the seal of the living God' upon the foreheads of God's servants as the mark of divine ownership and protection (Ezek. 9:1-4; Eph. 4:30; 2 Tim. 2:19), and so his first care is to prevent the angels of the winds from unleashing their judgements until the work of sealing is done. This sealing does not guarantee immunity from suffering (6:9), but though God's servants 'must suffer, many of them even unto death, they will finally be brought in safety out of all the woe into the eternal kingdom' (Beckwith).

vv. 4-8. And I heard the number of them that were sealed, a hundred and forty and four thousand, sealed out of every tribe of the children of Israel: of the tribe of Judah were sealed twelve thousand; of the tribe of Reuben twelve thousand; of the tribe of Gad twelve thousand; of the tribe of Asher twelve thousand; of the tribe of Naphtali twelve thousand; of the tribe of Manasseh twelve thousand; of the tribe of Simeon twelve thousand; of the tribe of Levi twelve thousand; of the tribe of Issachar twelve thousand; of the tribe of Zebulun twelve thousand; of the tribe of Joseph twelve thousand; of the tribe of Benjamin were sealed twelve thousand.

John does not witness the sealing, but he hears the number of those sealed — 144,000 consisting of 12,000 from each of the twelve tribes of Israel. This symbolic number represents the church as the true spiritual Israel (2:9; 3:9; 14:1; cf. Rom. 2:29; Gal. 3:29; 6:16). According to K. Rengstorf, 'twelve' indicates the divine will to save; 'thousands' stresses the size of the community; the 12,000 from each tribe 'brings out the orderly nature of the divine action and the perfection of the result' and the total number 'attests the absolute unity of those who are sealed' (*TDNT*, Vol. II, p.324). That ethnic Israel is not in view is confirmed by the irregular listing of the tribes. Judah is placed first as the Messiah's own tribe, Dan is omitted, Levi is included as an ordinary tribe and Joseph replaces Ephraim. Lenski observes that the two parts of this chapter constitute *'the revelation of the church. Sealed — Glorified!* This is to be our picture and vision of *the church.* It is transcendent.'

v.9. **After these things I saw, and behold, a great multitude, which no man could number, out of every nation, and of all tribes and peoples and tongues, standing before the throne and before the Lamb, arrayed in white robes, and palms in their hands . . .**

'After these things' introduces a fresh aspect of the vision as the scene shifts from earth to heaven. This preview of the final bliss of the redeemed is the logical sequel to the sealing of the 144,000. In John's vision the glorified church is revealed as a cosmopolitan body, for the vast throng which cannot be counted is drawn from every tribe and nation and made one in Christ (5:9). The saints stand accepted in the place of honour before the throne of God and before the Lamb, clothed in 'white robes' (v. 14) and with 'palms' in their hands (John 12:13), symbols which denote the purity and victory that is theirs by grace alone.

v.10. **. . . and they cry with a great voice, saying, Salvation unto our God who sitteth on the throne, and unto the Lamb.**

As with one voice, the great multitude of the redeemed ascribe their deliverance to the sovereign will of God and the sacrifice of the Lamb. 'Salvation unto our God' means that 'The praise and honour due for our salvation belongs to God, since he is the Cause of our salvation' (Plummer).

vv.11, 12. **And all the angels were standing round about the throne, and about the elders and the four living creatures; and they fell before the throne on their faces, and worshipped God, saying, Amen: Blessing, and glory, and wisdom, and thanksgiving, and honour, and power, and might, be unto our God for ever and ever. Amen.**

The view that the elders and the four living beings are angelic powers is supported by the fact that they join in the worship offered by all the angels around the throne (see comment on 4:4 and 4:6). The angels' first 'Amen' confirms the praise of the redeemed (v. 10), before they add their own tribute to God in a sevenfold doxology similar to that addressed to the Lamb in 5:12. God is praised as the fount of all the *blessing, glory* and *wisdom* which are so conspicuously displayed in the salvation of men (cf. Eph. 3:10), and is therefore the One to whom all the *thanksgiving* and *honour* belong for the exercise of his *power* and *might* in this great work of grace. 'For ever and ever' puts this adoration 'into the realm of eternal verities' (Morris) and the final 'Amen' sets the seal upon the truth just confessed.

vv.13, 14. **And one of the elders answered, saying unto me, These that are arrayed in the white robes, who are they, and whence came they? And I say unto him, My lord, thou knowest. And he said to me, These are they that come out of the great tribulation, and they washed their robes, and made them white in the blood of the Lamb.**

One of the elders interprets the vision by anticipating John's unspoken questions concerning the white-robed multitude (cf. 5:5). 'My lord' is the language of reverent regard for a heavenly being, but not that of worship (19:10; 22:8, 9). 'Thou knowest' is at once a confession of ignorance and a plea for enlightenment.

'And he said to me, "These are they who have come out of the

great tribulation" ' (RSV). This translation is preferable, since the ASV could be taken as implying that those whom John saw were still coming out of tribulation, whereas from the future standpoint of the vision the number of the redeemed is complete. Here 'the great tribulation' does not refer to any particular time of suffering, but includes all the afflictions through which the saints have passed on their way to glory (Acts 14:22). 'This tribulation is now completed and past, and is therefore referred to as "the great tribulation" ' (Plummer).

'And they washed their robes, and made them white in the blood of the Lamb.' This striking language applies to all believers alike, and there is nothing in the context to support the strange notion that it refers only to martyrs. By his sacrifice Christ merited salvation for his people, but the benefits won by that death must be appropriated by faith, and the aorist verbs here look back to the time on earth when they washed and whitened their robes in the blood of the Lamb. 'This blood and nothing else in the universe whitens us so that we may stand before God' (Lenski).

v. 15. **Therefore are they before the throne of God; and they serve him day and night in his temple: and he that sitteth on the throne shall spread his tabernacle over them.**

Because of this washing ('therefore'), the redeemed are before the throne of God, which is not only a place of safety but also of service. For heaven is the sanctuary in which they all constantly offer to God the priestly service of worship (5:10). The elder's concluding words depict the final bliss of God's people in a series of beautiful images (vv. 15-17). The promise that God 'shall spread his tabernacle over them' means that he will shelter his people from all harm by the glory ('Shekinah') of his abiding presence (21:3; Ezek. 37:27).

v. 16. **They shall hunger no more, neither thirst any more; neither** shall the sun strike upon them, nor any heat.

Blessed relief is promised from the privations suffered by Christ's faithful witnesses on earth. They shall be delivered from the inward pangs of hunger and thirst and from those outward trials which are symbolized by the scorching heat of the sun (Isa. 49:10). But these negatives also imply the satisfaction of all their needs (for food and drink, see John 6:35; for divine protection, see previous verse).

v.17. **For the Lamb that is in the midst of the throne shall be their shepherd, and shall guide them unto fountains of waters of life: and God shall wipe away every tear from their eyes.**

The Lamb as *Shepherd* may seem to be a surprising reversal of rôles, but as the Saviour of his blood-bought flock, he alone has the authority 'to guide them unto fountains of waters of life' (Ps. 23:1, 2; John 10:14). This figure promises the complete satisfaction of every need, even though the heavenly reality it represents is beyond our present understanding (1 Cor. 13:12). The state of glory will also be marked by the absence of all suffering and sorrow. The tender assurance that 'God shall wipe away every tear from their eyes' is taken from Isa. 25:8 (cf. 21:4). Words like these 'must sound as a divine music in the ears of the persecuted. God will comfort as a mother comforts' (J. M. S. Baljon).

Section 3
The seven trumpets of judgement

Revelation 8

As the Lamb opens the seventh seal, seven angels prepare to blow the seven trumpets of judgement in response to the prayers of the saints (vv. 1-5). After a description of the destruction wrought by the first four trumpets, a flying eagle warns that three fearful woes are yet to come (vv. 6-13).

vv.1, 2. And when he opened the seventh seal, there followed a silence in heaven about the space of half an hour. And I saw the seven angels that stand before God; and there were given unto them seven trumpets.

The opening of the seventh seal cannot follow the sixth in chronological sequence, because the contents of that seal portrayed the final day of wrath (6:12-17). The seven trumpets rather serve to introduce a series of judgements which are synchronous with those of the seals. Hence the vision covers the same ground again, but from a different point of view. The calamities described are typical judgements which recur throughout this dispensation, and should not be regarded as symbolizing particular events.

When the Lamb opened the seventh seal, there was a dramatic pause for about half an hour as the praise of the heavenly hosts was hushed in dread anticipation of the judgements to follow. John then saw that seven trumpets were given to 'the seven angels' that stand before God. The definite article points to a specific group of angels, who are possibly to be identified with

the seven angels of the Presence whose names are given in
1 Enoch 20:2-8 as Uriel, Raphael, Raguel, Michael (12:7;
Jude 9), Sariel, Gabriel (Luke 1:19) and Remiel. As the blowing
of trumpets signalled the fall of Jericho (Josh. 6:13), so those
assigned to the angels herald the 'end-time' judgements of God
(vv. 7-12; 9:1, 12; 11:15).

vv.3, 4. **And another angel came and stood over the altar, having
a golden censer; and there was given unto him much incense, that
he should add it unto the prayers of all the saints upon the golden
altar which was before the throne. And the smoke of the incense,
with the prayers of the saints, went up before God out of the
angel's hand.**

Another angel with a golden censer next appears on the scene, and
John saw that 'there was given unto him' much incense to offer
with the prayers of all the saints upon the altar of incense before
the throne (6:9). The angel is neither a mediator nor an inter-
cessor. He does not bring his own offering, but is given 'much
incense' and this symbol 'represents the intercession of Christ for
his church, which adds power and efficacy to the prayers of the
church' (Lenski). For it is only as the prayers of the saints are
purified by Christ's intercession that they ascend to God as a
fragrant offering.

v.5. **And the angel taketh the censer; and he filled it with the
fire of the altar, and cast it upon the earth: and there followed
thunders, and voices, and lightnings, and an earthquake.**

Having emptied the censer of incense, the angel takes it again in
order to fulfil another office. It is to be used now, not for the
offering of prayers, but for the work of judgement. He fills the
censer with fire from the altar, and casts its contents upon the
earth (Ezek. 10:2). This is a partial answer to the cry of the
martyrs for justice (6:10), and it means that 'the prayers of the

saints return to the earth in wrath' (Swete). The awesome portents that follow — thunders, voices of the storm, lightnings and earthquake — underline the power of God which is about to be manifested in his righteous judgements (cf. Exod. 19:16-25).

v.6. **And the seven angels that had the seven trumpets prepared themselves to sound.**

The seven angels know that these portents are the signal for them to play their part in the great drama, and they prepare to sound their trumpets to 'usher in the judgements which shall fulfil the prayers of God's people' (Beckwith). For the vindication of the saints calls for retribution on the wicked (cf. comment on 6:10).

v.7. **And the first sounded, and there followed hail and fire, mingled with blood, and they were cast upon the earth: and the third part of the earth was burnt up, and the third part of the trees was burnt up, and all green grass was burnt up.**

The first four trumpets form a group of warning judgements directed against the sources of life which men in their blindness take for granted. These judgements resemble the Egyptian plagues which were sent to move Pharaoh to repentance, but, as in the case of their prototypes, they only serve to harden the hearts of the wicked (9:20, 21). Hail and fire recall the fourth plague (Exod. 9:23-26), while the phrase 'mingled with blood' adds to the dramatic intensity of the picture (Ezek. 38:22). In the third part of the earth which was affected by this judgement, the fire burnt all the grass and a third of the trees. John's purpose is to show that there are no natural disasters in a world which is governed by God. The curse does not come without a cause. The trumpets thus depict God's judgements 'on the world, not the trials of the Church. The Church is the true Israel which exists uninjured by these manifestations of God's wrath in the midst of the world of Egyptian wickedness' (Plummer).

vv.8, 9. And the second angel sounded, and as it were a great mountain burning with fire was cast into the sea: and the third part of the sea became blood; and there died the third part of the creatures which were in the sea, even they that had life; and the third part of the ships was destroyed.

When the second trumpet sounded something that looked like a blazing mountain was cast into the sea, turning a third of it to blood. This brought death to all marine life and destroyed the ships in that part of the sea. Here the turning of the water into blood and the destruction of the fish bring to mind the first Egyptian plague (Exod. 7:20, 21). But to attempt to interpret the blazing mountain in terms of volcanic eruptions, like that of Vesuvius in A.D. 79, is to misunderstand the nature of such apocalyptic images. The evident meaning of the terrible picture is that the sea can also be used by God to punish and warn mankind. For if the loss of lives and property in all the sea disasters throughout the centuries could be calculated, this vision would not seem at all extravagant.

vv.10, 11. And the third angel sounded, and there fell from heaven a great star, burning as a torch, and it fell upon the third part of the rivers, and upon the fountains of the waters; and the name of the star is called Wormwood: and the third part of the waters became wormwood; and many men died of the waters, because they were made bitter.

At the third trumpet-blast a great fiery star called Wormwood fell upon a third part of the rivers and springs (Jer. 9:15). This made the fresh water as bitter as wormwood, in contrast to the miracles which sweetened bitter waters (cf. Exod. 15:25; 2 Kings 2:21). It is off the mark to say that womwood is not actually poisonous. The expression simply means that the waters became charged with sorrow and disaster, so that many died through floods, drought, water pollution, pestilence etc. The star points to 'the awe-striking nature of the punishment, and is indicative of the fact that the judgement is the act of God, and proceeds directly from heaven, and is not to be attributed to merely natural circumstances' (Plummer).

v.12. **And the fourth angel sounded, and the third part of the sun was smitten, and the third part of the moon, and the third part of the stars; that the third part of them should be darkened, and the day should not shine for the third part of it, and the night in like manner.**

At the sound of the fourth trumpet the heavenly luminaries are so darkened that they cease to give any light for a third of the day and night. This judgement recalls the ninth Egyptian plague (Exod. 10:21-23). The first part of the verse seems to mean that the intensity of light was reduced by a third, whereas the second part indicates that there was total darkness for a third of the day and night. However, it should be obvious that John is painting a picture and not writing a treatise on astronomy! The darkness prefigures the doom of the ungodly (Isa. 13:10), and is also the prelude to the new exodus of God's people from under the hands of their oppressors (cf. 11:8; Luke 21:28). In an age which looks to the stars for guidance, this verse reminds us that God exercises complete control over the solar system. 'God can turn even the benign influences of the sun and planets into means for the destruction of man. In the countless evils which have their origin in the excess or defect of the power of the sun, we may see an illustration of the fulfilment of this judgement' (Plummer).

v.13. **And I saw, and I heard an eagle, flying in mid heaven, saying with a great voice, Woe, woe, woe, for them that dwell on earth, by reason of the other voices of the trumpet of the three angels, who are yet to sound.**

The bird of prey John next sees flying in mid-heaven is an omen of worse to come. The eagle proclaims a triple woe 'for them that

dwell on earth' (i.e. the wicked, as can be seen from 9:4, 20),
because of the three trumpets yet to sound.

Revelation 9

*The woes inflicted by the fifth and sixth trumpets attack men
directly. The former of these releases a swarm of satanic locusts
from the bottomless pit which torment men for five months
(vv. 1-12). The latter looses four angels with a vast army of
fiendish horsemen to kill a third of mankind. But those unaffec-
ted by this judgement still refused to repent of their wickedness
(vv. 13-21).*

v.1. **And the fifth angel sounded, and I saw a star from heaven
fallen unto the earth: and there was given to him the key of the
pit of the abyss.**

At the sounding of the fifth trumpet John saw a star which had
fallen from heaven to earth. From what follows (v. 11), it appears
that the star is a fallen angel named 'Apollyon' (i.e. Destroyer),
who is permitted 'to exercise malicious power on earth in furtherance of divine judgement' (Moffatt). There is a vast difference
between this fallen angel who 'was given' the key of the abyss,
and the angel of 20:1, who descends from heaven with this key
in his hand as the willing agent of the divine purpose (Caird).
'The abyss' is the abode of demons before the final judgement
(Luke 8:31), and the reservoir of evil from which the worst
dangers arise (cf. 11:7; 17:8).

v.2. **And he opened the pit of the abyss; and there went up a**

smoke out of the pit, as the smoke of a great furnace; and the sun
and the air were darkened by reason of the smoke of the pit.

When the fallen angel unlocked the shaft of the abyss, there rose
up a dense cloud of smoke like that from a great furnace, obscur-
ing the sun and befouling the air with its noxious fumes. The
verse presents a vivid picture of the pervasive power of evil,
'which clouds men's minds and darkens their understandings'
(Plummer).

v.3. And out of the smoke came forth locusts upon the earth;
and power was given them, as the scorpions of the earth have
power.

Out of the smoke John saw a swarm of locusts come upon the
earth, but they were unlike ordinary locusts which merely devour
all the vegetation, as in the Egyptian plague and the prophecies
of punishment in Joel (Exod. 10:1-20; Joel 1:2-2:11). For these
fearsome creatures were given the authority to inflict torment
upon the ungodly with their scorpion-like stings (vv. 5, 10). 'The
scorpion takes its place with the snake and other creatures hostile
to man, and with them symbolizes the forces of spiritual evil
which are active in the world' (Swete).

v.4. And it was said unto them that they should not hurt the
grass of the earth, neither any green thing, neither any tree, but
only such men as have not the seal of God on their foreheads.

The locusts were not permitted to harm the vegetation of the
earth, but only the men who had not the seal of God on their
foreheads (7:1-8). As the Israelites were protected from the
plagues which punished the Egyptians (Exod. 8:22; 9:4, 26;
10:23; 11:7), so the new Israel is exempted from the torments
arising from the abyss. This means that the children of God
are strangers to the spiritual torments that plague the wicked

(Luke 10:19). 'No real injury can happen to them; pain and death might be encountered, but all things work together for their higher good . . . No plague can hurt those who have the seal of God on their foreheads. A plague from which those whose way is through tribulation are exempt can hardly be a physical one' (Carpenter).

vv.5, 6. **And it was given them that they should not kill them, but that they should be tormented five months: and their torment was as the torment of a scorpion, when it striketh a man. And in those days men shall seek death, and shall in no wise find it; and they shall desire to die, and death fleeth from them.**

The power of the locusts is limited by the will of God to a period of five months, perhaps corresponding to the natural life-span of these creatures. A torment which lasts for five months is a long time, but is still of limited duration. It is clear from verse 6 that the anguish inflicted by the locusts' scorpion-like stings is restricted to the present life of the ungodly, or they would not desire death to release them from it. 'The withholding of death, instead of being an alleviation, is really a refinement of torture; so infernal is the pain, that the sufferer's crave, but crave in vain, for death' (Moffatt).

vv.7-10. **And the shapes of the locusts were like unto horses prepared for war; and upon their heads as it were crowns like unto gold, and their faces were as men's faces. And they had hair as the hair of women, and the teeth were as the teeth of lions. And they had breastplates, as it were breastplates of iron; and the sound of their wings was as the sound of chariots, of many horses rushing to war. And they have tails like unto scorpions, and stings; and in their tails is their power to hurt men five months.**

John's description of the demonic appearance of these locusts

shows that the attempt to compare them with an ordinary swarm
of locusts is quite misguided. 'They are locusts, but they have the
malice of scorpions; they advance like horse-soldiers to battle;
they wear crowns; they bear a resemblance to men; there is
something womanlike also in their appearance, and in their
voracity they are as lions. The exigencies of the symbolism are
quite beyond the features of the ordinary locust: the sacred
writer shows us a plague in which devastation, malice, king-like
authority, intelligence, seductiveness, fierceness, strength, meet
together under one directing spirit, to torment men' (Carpenter).

v.11. **They have over them as king the angel of the abyss: his
name in Hebrew is Abaddon, and in the Greek tongue he hath
the name Apollyon.**

In contrast to ordinary locusts (Prov. 30:27), these locusts have
the angel of the abyss as their king, for they obey his orders and
do his work (cf. v. 1). John knows the name of this fallen angel:
it is in Hebrew *Abaddon* and in Greek *Apollyon,* meaning the
Destroyer. He is not Satan but one of his minions; Satan himself
does not appear before the vision of the woman and the dragon
in ch. 12.

v.12. **The first Woe is past: behold, there come yet two Woes
hereafter.**

This dramatic announcement marks the end of the first woe and
warns that two more are yet to come (8:13; 9:12; 11:14).

vv.13-15. **And the sixth angel sounded, and I heard a voice from
the horns of the golden altar which is before God, one saying to
the sixth angel that had the trumpet, Loose the four angels that
are bound at the great river Euphrates. And the four angels were
loosed, that had been prepared for the hour and day and month**

and year, that they should kill the third part of men.

The voice that John heard commanding the sixth angel to release the second woe came from the horns of the golden altar of incense (Exod. 30:2), which shows that this judgement is in response to the prayers of the saints (cf. 6:9, 10; 8:3-5). The four evil angels who were kept bound at the Euphrates were not permitted to embark upon their strictly limited mission of destruction ('that they should kill the third part of men', cf. v. 18) until the exact moment determined by God. There is symbolic significance in the direction from which the judgement is launched, because the world powers God used to punish apostate Israel for her idolatry came from beyond the river Euphrates (Isa. 7:20). Thus a corrupt civilization which indulges in the same sin will incur the same judgement. 'The aim of the plague is to exhibit the death-working power of false thoughts, false customs, false beliefs, and to rouse men to forsake the false worships, worldliness, and self-indulgence into which they had fallen (vv. 20, 21)' (Carpenter).

vv. 16-19. **And the number of the armies of the horsemen was twice ten thousand times ten thousand: I heard the number of them. And thus I saw the horses in the vision, and them that sat on them, having breastplates as of fire and of hyacinth and of brimstone: and the heads of the horses are as the heads of lions; and out of their mouths proceedeth fire and smoke and brimstone. By these three plagues was the third part of men killed, by the fire and the smoke and the brimstone, which proceeded out of their mouths. For the power of the horses is in their mouth, and in their tails: for their tails are like unto serpents, and have heads; and with them they hurt.**

This is the only place in the book where John specifically states that he is describing what he saw in a vision, because only thus could he perceive the vast forces which were armed with supernatural powers to torment and kill a third of mankind. He saw an

immense host of two hundred million horsemen, the colour of
whose breastplates matched the three plagues of fire, smoke
('hyacinth' = dark blue) and sulphur that proceeded from the
lionlike mouths of their fiendish mounts. These diabolical animals
also had tails like serpents, with which to torment their victims.
The whole judgement 'portrays the spiritual evils which afflict
the ungodly in this life . . . The number of such inflictions is,
indeed, great enough to be described as "two myriads of myriads"
(v. 16); they destroy a part, but not the greater part (v. 15, "the
third part") of men; and yet how largely they fail to bring men
to repentance! Such punishment is a foretaste of hell, as seems to
be foreshadowed in the "fire and smoke and brimstone" of
verses 17, 18' (Plummer).

vv.20, 21. **And the rest of mankind, who were not killed with
these plagues, repented not of the works of their hands, that they
should not worship demons, and the idols of gold, and of silver,
and of brass, and of stone, and of wood; which can neither see,
nor hear, nor walk: and they repented not of their murders, nor
of their sorceries, nor of their fornication, nor of their thefts.**

The majority who escaped this terrible judgement might have
been expected to take warning from the fate of their fellows,
and to become servants of God and of Christ. But they were so
far from doing this that they did not even repent of their idolatry.
Such repentance would have led them 'to abandon the worship
of unclean spirits and of the idols that represented them' (Swete).
(Cf. Deut. 32:17; 1 Cor. 10:20.) These idols are scornfully
described as 'the works of their hands', because the gods they
make from existing materials like gold and silver 'can neither see,
nor hear, nor walk' (Ps. 115:5-7; Dan. 5:23). The further charge
of verse 21 shows that they were no more willing to repent of
their evil deeds than of their idolatry, for false worship leads to
every kind of wickedness (Rom. 1:18-32). John later reveals that
the lake of fire awaits all who persist in idolatry and the sins that
accompany it (21:8).

Revelation 10

John sees a mighty angel descend from heaven with a little book in his hand and hears him announce that the mystery of God will shortly be fulfilled. The angel gives John the book to eat. First it tastes sweet, but then turns bitter because of the woes it contains (vv. 1-11).

v.1. And I saw another strong angel coming down out of heaven, arrayed with a cloud; and the rainbow was upon his head, and his face was as the sun, and his feet as pillars of fire . . .

Apparently John is now back on earth, for he sees a mighty angel coming down from heaven. The description of this angel has led some to identify him with Christ, but John could never introduce Christ as 'another angel' (cf. 8:3). The angel's appearance points to his celestial dignity. He is clad in a cloud, 'the vehicle in which heavenly beings descend and ascend' (Swete); the rainbow upon his head gives the church further assurance of God's covenant faithfulness (see note on 4:3); while his face shone like the sun, and his feet were like pillars of fire. 'The last two clauses express the same idea, viz. the bright and glorious appearance of the angel. God's glory is reflected in his messenger, as formerly it was in Moses (Exod. 34:29, 30)' (Plummer).

v.2. . . . and he had in his hand a little book open: and he set his right foot upon the sea, and his left upon the earth . . .

The angel had a little book which lay open in his hand, thus showing that its contents were to be made known to men. No great stress should be placed on the diminutive. The 'little' book contained prophecies of world-wide significance (vv. 6, 11), yet it was small enough for John to eat (cf. Ezek. 2:8-3:3). In this vision the angel appears as a colossal figure, who bestrides sea and land, 'and cries with a loud voice, because his message is addressed to the whole world' (Beckwith).

vv.3, 4. . . . and he cried with a great voice, as a lion roareth: and when he cried, the seven thunders uttered their voices. And when the seven thunders uttered their voices, I was about to write: and I heard a voice from heaven saying, Seal up the things which the seven thunders uttered, and write them not.

The shout of the angel was like the roar of a lion (Hosea 11:10; Amos 3:8); 'and when he shouted, the seven thunders spoke' (NEB). John evidently understood the meaning of this utterance, and was just about to write it down when a voice from heaven (presumably the voice of God or Christ) forbids him to reveal what he has heard (cf. Dan. 12:4). 'The Seer's enforced reticence witnesses to the fragmentary character of even apocalyptic disclosures. The Seer himself received more than he was at liberty to communicate' (Swete). (Cf. 2 Cor. 12:4.) It is thus pointless to speculate on the nature of what is purposely concealed from us (Deut. 29:29).

vv.5, 6. And the angel that I saw standing upon the sea and upon the earth lifted up his right hand to heaven, and sware by him that liveth for ever and ever, who created the heaven and the things that are therein, and the earth and the things that are therein, and the sea and the things that are therein, that there shall be delay no longer . . .

The angel then lifted up his right hand to heaven (Deut. 32:40;

Dan. 12:7), and solemnly swore by the eternal God, who is the Creator of all things, that there should be no more delay in the fulfilment of the divine purpose (v. 7).

1. Because God is *eternal,* he is certain to fulfil what he has planned. The 'problem' of evil cannot baffle or outwit the one who is a stranger to improvization and frustration (Prov. 21:30).

2. Because God is *the Creator,* he is sure to accomplish the purpose he had in creating the world (4:11). The sovereignty of God over the whole creation means that all things must contribute to his glory and work together for the final good of his people (Rom. 8:28).

v. 7. . . . but in the days of the voice of the seventh angel, when he is about to sound, then is finished the mystery of God, according to the good tidings which he declared to his servants the prophets.

The angel proclaims that there shall be no further delay (v. 6), but within the period to be introduced by the sounding of the seventh trumpet the mystery of God will be accomplished (11:15-18). 'The mystery of God' is the eternal purpose of God, which was once kept secret but is now revealed (Rom. 16:25, 26). The consummation of this mystery includes the final judgement of the wicked, and 'the full salvation of the saints in the perfected kingdom' (Beckwith). This will be no 'surprise' ending, but the fulfilment of the good tidings that God gave 'to his servants the prophets' (Amos 3:7). The promise given here is 'good news indeed for the fainting Christian, for it tells of the end of his trials and the overthrow of his enemies' (Plummer).

v. 8. And the voice which I heard from heaven, I heard it again speaking with me, and saying, Go, take the book which is open in the hand of the angel that standeth upon the sea and upon the earth.

This is the same heavenly voice that forbade John to write down what the seven thunders uttered (v. 4). He now hears another command requiring the same prompt obedience. He is to approach the angel and take the book that lies open in his hand.

vv.9, 10. **And I went unto the angel, saying unto him that he should give me the little book. And he saith unto me, Take it, and eat it up; and it shall make thy belly bitter, but in thy mouth it shall be sweet as honey. And I took the little book out of the angel's hand, and ate it up; and it was in my mouth sweet as honey: and when I had eaten it, my belly was made bitter.**

The angel instructs John to take the little book and eat it up, but warns him that it will be bitter to digest, even though it will taste as sweet as honey (Ps. 19:10). John's experience proved to be similar to that of Ezekiel, who found that God's Word tasted sweet (Ezek. 3:3), but because the scroll was filled with woe his mood was soon changed to one of bitterness (cf. Ezek. 2:10; 3:14). Hence the physical bitterness John felt matched the terrible nature of the judgement he had to announce (v. 11). 'The true preacher of God's Word will faithfully proclaim the denunciations of the wicked it contains. But he does not do this with fierce glee. The more his heart is filled with the love of God, the more certain it is that the telling forth of "woes" will be a bitter experience' (Morris).

v.11. **And they say unto me, Thou must prophesy again over many peoples and nations and tongues and kings.**

'They say' is rather strange, but is probably the equivalent of the passive 'it was said' (cf. RSV: 'I was told').

'Thou must prophesy again concerning many peoples and nations and tongues and kings' (ASV margin). The fourfold enumeration shows that the prophecy embraces the whole of mankind. The burden of woe that concerns so many is laid upon John by the 'must' of divine necessity. It is to be done 'again', because he has already 'to some extent set forth God's will in the earlier part of the book; and he is now required to proceed with the delivery of his message' (Plummer).

Revelation 11

John is told to measure the temple and count the worshippers (vv. 1, 2). After God's two witnesses have prophesied for 1260 days, they are killed by the beast from the abyss, but rise again and ascend to heaven (vv. 3-13). At the seventh trumpet blast, the proclamation of Christ's victory in heaven is followed by the outpouring of God's wrath upon the world (vv. 14-19).

v.1. **And there was given me a reed like unto a rod: and one said, Rise, and measure the temple of God, and the altar, and them that worship therein.**

John is given a reed like a measuring rod, and is instructed to measure the inner sanctuary of God, the altar of incense (8:3) and those who worship therein (cf. Ezek. 40). The last clause is significant, for only the priests were allowed to enter the Holy of Holies in the temple at Jerusalem, but now all believers enjoy immediate access to God. Hence this is a picture of God's new temple, the church (1 Cor. 3:16; Eph. 2:19-22). The church is measured to show that it will be protected and preserved from spiritual danger, though not from physical suffering, and the assurance thus conveyed corresponds to the sealing of the 144,000 (7:1-8).

v.2. **And the court which is without the temple leave without, and measure it not; for it hath been given unto the nations: and**

the holy city shall they tread under foot forty and two months.

From the aspect of its eternal security the church is preserved inviolate (v. 1), but in regard to its earthly existence it is subject to persecution by 'the heathen' (i.e. 'the nations' or 'the Gentiles'). So John is forbidden to measure the outer court of the temple, because God has given the heathen the power to trample on 'the holy city' (i.e. the church viewed as the new Jerusalem) for 'forty and two months'. The time limit which is set for this trial is derived from Daniel 7:25, and refers to the three and a half years of terror under Antiochus Epiphanes when the temple at Jerusalem was desecrated (June 168 to December 165 B.C.). In this book, forty-two months (13:5), 1260 days (v. 3; 12:6) and 'a time, and times, and half a time' (12:14) are equivalent designations for the same period. 'By comparing these passages with the present context we get the equation: the duration of the triumph of the Gentiles = the duration of the prophesying of the Two Witnesses, = the duration of the Woman's sojourn in the wilderness. The time-limit serves of course no further purpose than to synchronize the several periods, and to compare them with the greatest crisis through which the Jewish people passed between the Exile and the Fall of Jerusalem' (Swete).

v.3. **And I will give unto my two witnesses, and they shall prophesy a thousand two hundred and threescore days, clothed in sackcloth**.

The two witnesses are appointed by God to prophesy for 1260 days, and are clothed in sackcloth because their message is a call to repentance (Matt. 11:21). These witnesses are not actual men like Moses and Elijah, even though they exercise similar powers (vv. 5, 6). They are rather a collective symbol of the church, for two witnesses were necessary to give competent legal testimony (Deut. 17:6; 19:15). The purpose of the vision is to promote obedience: it is a summons to the church to bear witness to the truth before a hostile world (cf. 2:10).

v.4. **These are the two olive trees and the two candlesticks, standing before the Lord of the earth.**

The two witnesses are now identified as the two olive trees and two lampstands that stand before the Lord of the earth (Zech. 4:2-14). It is because the church is constantly supplied with the oil of the Spirit that the lamp of witness is not quenched by the opposition of evil men. In Zechariah the two olive trees represent Zerubbabel the prince and Joshua the priest, who thus symbolize the royal and priestly prerogatives of the church (1:6; 5:10; 20:6). But instead of Zechariah's single lampstand, there are two lampstands here to match the two witnesses. These lampstands depict the whole church, and not just a minority of martyrs. For all believers are called to be faithful witnesses, not fearing what man can do, as befits those who are privileged to stand 'before the Lord of the earth'.

v.5. **And if any man desireth to hurt them, fire proceedeth out of their mouth and devoureth their enemies; and if any man shall desire to hurt them, in this manner must he be killed.**

John next proceeds to show that those who oppose God's witnesses only succeed in bringing destruction upon themselves (vv. 5, 6). There is an allusion to Elijah, who called down fire from heaven on the soldiers sent to arrest him (2 Kings 1:10-12), but here the fire comes out of the mouths of the witnesses. This means that their enemies are inevitably killed by the power of God's Word (Jer. 5:14). 'The Word in the mouth of the Lord's prophet-witnesses may be scorned but it is not an empty sound. Its judgements are fire that devours its enemies' (Lenski).

v.6. **These have the power to shut the heaven, that it rain not during the days of their prophesy; and they have power over the waters to turn them into blood, and to smite the earth with every plague, as often as they shall desire.**

These witnesses also have the same power as Elijah to shut the heavens to prevent rain during the time of their prophecy (1 Kings 17:1). And like Moses they can also turn water into blood and inflict whatever plague they wish (Exod. 7:20-25). John's purpose here may be to express 'the truth that God's servants in the new dispensation have just as great resources as did Moses and Elijah in the old' (Morris).

v. 7. **And when they shall have finished their testimony, the beast that cometh up out of the abyss shall make war with them, and overcome them, and kill them.**

The witnesses are immortal until they have completed their testimony, but at the end of the period determined by God they are killed by the beast that 'comes up' from the abyss (13:1; 17:8). The present tense of the verb points to a permanent attribute of the beast, for the abyss is the place of its origin and the source of its power (9:1). The beast appears to represent those antichristian powers in the world which seek to silence the church's witness. However, the fact that the beast finally prevails over the two witnesses does not mean that the whole church will be martyred. John's intention is to show that the church will experience increasing opposition from the power of Satan, which will result 'in the apparent triumph of the forces of evil. But the triumph will be brief; it will but usher in the end and the final subjugation of the devil' (Plummer).

v. 8. **And their dead bodies lie in the street of the great city, which spiritually is called Sodom and Egypt, where also their Lord was crucified.**

In a display of the utmost contempt, the dead bodies of the witnesses are left unburied in the street of the great city, which is stained with the blood of all the prophets (Matt. 23:35; Luke 13:33). Thus Jerusalem, 'where also their Lord was crucified', is that secular city which has the character of Sodom and Egypt: it is a place of uncleanness and the oppressor of the true people of God (Isa. 1:9, 10; Jer. 23:14). As such, it is the ignoble proto-type of the great city of Babylon (which in John's day was Rome), wherein was found 'the blood of prophets and of saints, and of all that have been slain upon the earth' (18:24).

v.9. **And from among the peoples and tribes and tongues and nations do men look upon their dead bodies three days and a half, and suffer not their dead bodies to be laid in a tomb.**

The unburied bodies of the witnesses are viewed by men of every race and nation. But the three and a half days of their humili-ation are a short period compared with the three and a half years of their ministry (v. 3). So the triumph of the ungodly is in fact very brief, though 'long enough to bear the semblance of being complete and final' (Swete).

v.10. **And they that dwell on the earth rejoice over them, and make merry; and they shall send gifts one to another; because these two prophets tormented them that dwell on the earth.**

The men of the world are jubilant at the death of the two prophets whose fearless testimony had tormented their consciences for so long (vv. 4, 5; cf. 1 Kings 18:17). In typical oriental fashion, they celebrate the festive occasion by sending gifts to one another (Esth. 9:19, 22). 'Such a sense of relief is not seldom felt by bad men when a preacher of righteousness or a signal example of goodness is removed, though good breeding may prevent outward manifestation of joy' (Swete).

v.11. **And after the three days and a half the breath of life from God entered into them, and they stood upon their feet; and great fear fell upon them that beheld them.**

But the rejoicing of the wicked was short-lived, for after the three and a half days God sent the breath of life into the dead bodies of the witnesses, and they stood upon their feet (Ezek. 37:10). The spectators of their return to life were panic-stricken at the power of God thus displayed. The world has often celebrated the death of the church, only to see it rise again from the verge of extinction. 'Each such resurrection strikes consternation into the hearts of her oppressors' (Morris).

v.12. **And they heard a great voice from heaven saying unto them, Come up hither. And they went up into heaven in the cloud; and their enemies beheld them.**

A great voice then called the two witnesses to heaven, and they went up in full view of their enemies. The event John describes is clearly no secret rapture; God's vindication of his persecuted people will be visible to all. But this final triumph of the church 'has been partly anticipated in the sight of the world by the tribute paid to the victims of a persecution, sometimes within a few years after their dishonour and death . . . paganism saw the men it had hated and killed called up to heaven before its eyes' (Swete).

v.13. **And in that hour there was a great earthquake, and the tenth part of the city fell; and there were killed in the earthquake seven thousand persons: and the rest were affrighted, and gave glory to the God of heaven.**

The hour of victory for the church is the hour of judgement for the world. But here John describes only the first shock of the final catastrophe, because he is concerned to stress the terrified reaction of the rest of humanity (cf. the parallel scene in 6:15-17). The revelation of God's irresistible might fills them with terror, and they are forced to acknowledge his sovereignty. Men will give glory to God when it is too late for them to repent. Indeed such repentance is impossible without the witness of the Word. Hence the rapture of the church is the end of all hope for the world.

v.14. **The second Woe is past: behold, the third Woe cometh quickly.**

It is surprising that the announcement of the third woe is not followed by a description of the final judgement. But the seventh trumpet 'does something greater, it pictures a scene in heaven *after* the judgement and lets us hear what the judgement signifies for God and his Christ, for the obdurate world, and for Christ's prophets and saints' (Lenski).

v.15. **And the seventh angel sounded; and there followed great voices in heaven, and they said, The kingdom of the world is become the kingdom of our Lord, and of his Christ: and he shall reign for ever and ever.**

When the seventh trumpet sounded, John heard the voices of the angelic hosts in heaven proclaiming the final triumph of the kingdom of God. They rejoice that the kingdom of the world has become the kingdom of their Lord (i.e. God) and of his Christ (i.e. 'his anointed', cf. Ps. 2:2). This means that the world, which was once under the usurped dominion of Satan, has now at last passed into the hands of its true owner and king (Swete).

'**And he shall reign for ever and ever.**' Although the subject of the verb is God, the joint sovereignty of Christ is implied in the preceding phrase 'and of his Christ' (Beckwith).

v.16. **And the four and twenty elders, who sit before God on their thrones, fell upon their faces and worshipped God . . .**

As already noted (see comment on 4:4), the twenty-four elders are a superior order of angelic beings, and are not to be identified with the redeemed. N. B. Stonehouse observes that they refer to 'the saints' and 'them that destroy the earth' with equal detachment (vv. 17, 18), and asks how one can account for this attitude, 'if we are meant to understand that the redeemed people of God, represented by the elders, are glorifying God for their own salvation?' (*Paul before the Areopagus and other New Testament Studies,* p.102).

vv.17, 18. . . . **saying, We give thee thanks, O Lord God, the Almighty, who art and who wast; because thou hast taken thy great power, and didst reign. And the nations were wroth, and thy wrath came, and the time of the dead to be judged, and the time to give their reward to thy servants the prophets, and to the saints, and to them that fear thy name, the small and the great; and to destroy them that destroy the earth.**

The song of the elders celebrates the final victory of God, who has demonstrated his great power and entered upon his triumphant reign (cf. NIV, RSV). It is significant that God is not here praised as the one 'who is to come' (cf. 1:8), because he has now come and decisively defeated the powers of evil. For the last fierce assault of the nations against the church has called down the wrath of God and ushered in the Day of Judgement. This is the day of *reward* for all God's people, both the small and the great, of whom the prophets are singled out for special mention. It is also the day of *retribution* for God's enemies. Those now bent on destroying the earth shall then justly be consigned to everlasting destruction. This clearly 'contradicts those who try to divide the judgement day into completely separate events' (Buis).

v.19. **And there was opened the temple of God that is in heaven; and there was seen in his temple the ark of his covenant; and** there followed lightnings, and voices, and thunders, and an earthquake, and great hail.

The divine response to this praise is seen in the opening of the heavenly sanctuary to disclose the ark of the covenant, which is the visible sign that God's covenant with his people has been fulfilled. The manifestation of God's grace is followed by the awesome tokens of his majesty and power, 'the solemn salvos, so to speak, of the artillery of Heaven' (Alford).

Section 4

The woman and the dragon

Revelation 12

The woman with child is threatened by the dragon, but the child is taken up to God (vv. 1-6). Michael and his angels war against the dragon and victory is proclaimed in heaven (vv. 7-12). But the dragon continues to persecute the woman on earth (vv. 13-17).

v.1. **And a great sign was seen in heaven: a woman arrayed with the sun, and the moon under her feet, and upon her head a crown of twelve stars . . .**

In this chapter we are shown the purpose which lies behind Satan's attacks upon the people of God. The great wonder John sees displayed in the sky is a woman whose appearance is dazzling. She is clothed with the sun, crowned with twelve stars and stands upon the moon. The description simply emphasizes the dignity of her position. The woman should be regarded as an ideal symbol of God's people in both dispensations. Many have noted the glaring contrast between the heavenly glory of the woman and the earthly glitter of the great harlot (17:4).

v.2. **. . . and she was with child; and she crieth out, travailing in birth, and in pain to be delivered.**

The woman is pictured as pregnant, and she cries in anguish as she labours to give birth to her child. This cry of travail fills the Old Testament as the chosen community longs for the advent of 'the seed of the woman' (Gen. 3:15; Isa. 26:17; Micah 4:9, 10; 5:2, 3). In Scripture no sharp dividing line is drawn between the true Israel and the new Israel, because the people of the promise are one people, whether they lived before or after the coming of Christ (Matt. 8:11; Rom. 4:16; Gal. 3:9).

v.3. **And there was seen another sign in heaven: and behold, a great red dragon, having seven heads and ten horns, and upon his heads seven diadems.**

The second sign John sees in the sky is a great red dragon with seven heads, which he later identifies as 'the old serpent, he that is called the Devil and Satan' (v. 9). The red colour of the dragon symbolizes his murderous character (John 8:44). On his seven heads are seven diadems, which are the symbols of his usurped dominion, while the ten horns indicate the completeness of his power over the kingdoms of the world (Dan. 7:7).

v.4. **And his tail draweth the third part of the stars of heaven, and did cast them to the earth: and the dragon standeth before the woman that is about to be delivered, that when she is delivered he may devour her child.**

The power of the dragon was such that the sweep of his tail was able to drag away a third of the stars of heaven and cast them to the earth (Dan. 8:10). This dramatic figure has the introductory function of illustrating the destructive power of the dragon, but the main purpose of the verse is to show that this power is directed against God's Messiah. Thus the dragon stands before the woman waiting to devour her child as soon as he is born. 'The pregnant woman is the church which is pregnant with the promise of the Messiah beginning with Genesis 3:15. Satan's one aim was "to devour" or destroy this Messiah' (Lenski).

v.5. **And she was delivered of a son, a man child, who is to rule all the nations with a rod of iron: and her child was caught up unto God, and unto his throne.**

The woman gives birth to a male child, who is clearly the Lord's anointed, for he is destined to rule the nations with a rod of iron (Ps. 2:9; cf. 19:15). Without referring to the earthly life, John passes straight from Christ's birth to the ascension, because he wishes to stress the fact that the dragon's plan was foiled by an act of divine power. The child was caught up to God, 'and unto his throne'. These words 'are added to emphasize the completeness of Satan's failure; the Messiah, so far from being destroyed, is caught up to a share in God's throne' (Beckwith).

v.6. **And the woman fled into the wilderness, where she hath a place prepared of God, that there they may nourish her a thousand two hundred and threescore days.**

Since the woman is now the object of the dragon's fury (v. 13), she flees to a refuge prepared by God in the wilderness, where she will be nourished for 1260 days (see comment on 11:2). The church is thus assured that she will be divinely protected and sustained throughout the short period of her testing on earth, just as the Israelites who fled from the Egyptian dragon (Ezek. 29:3) found safety and food in the wilderness.

vv.7, 8. **And there was war in heaven: Michael and his angels going forth to war with the dragon; and the dragon warred and his angels; and they prevailed not, neither was their place found any more in heaven.**

The next scene in the drama reveals the effect of Christ's victory in heaven. Michael, as the guardian angel of God's people (Dan. 10:13, 21; 12:1), leads an attack upon the dragon and his angels, which results in their defeat and expulsion from heaven (Luke

10:18). 'The reference here is to a definitive fall of Satan from heaven, so that he no longer has any access to God as accuser, 12:10' (W. Foerster, *TDNT*, Vol. III, p.157). In former times Satan could enter heaven as the accuser of God's people (Job. 1:6-12; Zech. 3:1, 2), but now that the price of their redemption has been paid he can do so no longer (v. 11; Rom. 8:34). But if the victory is really Christ's, why is Michael represented as the victor of the war in heaven? The answer is that Michael was only able to conquer in heaven in virtue of Christ's decisive conquest on earth (Col. 2:15). G. B. Caird helpfully likens Michael to the staff officer who is able to remove Satan's flag from the heavenly map because the officer in the field has won the real victory on Calvary.

v.9. **And the great dragon was cast down, the old serpent, he that is called the Devil and Satan, the deceiver of the whole world; he was cast down to the earth, and his angels were cast down with him.**

The identity of the dragon is here put beyond all doubt. He is called:
1. 'The old serpent', whose first act of deceit was to beguile Eve in the garden (Gen. 3:1-7);
2. 'The Devil', (which means 'slanderer') because he is the calumniator of God's servants, v. 10;
3. 'Satan' (which means 'adversary'), because he is the great enemy of mankind;
4. 'The deceiver of the whole world', which is blinded by his lies (2 Cor. 4:4).
   The ejection of Satan from heaven means that his fury is now directed against the church on earth (v. 13), but he is a defeated foe whose days are numbered and whose doom is sealed (20:10).

v.10. **And I heard a great voice in heaven, saying, Now is come the salvation, and the power, and the kingdom of our God, and** the authority of his Christ: for the accuser of our brethren is cast down, who accuseth them before our God day and night.

The great voice in heaven John hears is probably that of an angel, despite the reference to 'our brethren', for the angels are united with the redeemed in the kinship of mutual service (cf. 19:10). The voice announces the triumph of God's salvation, power and kingdom, in which Christ has assumed his right to rule, following his enthronement in heaven (v. 5). Nothing can now hinder the salvation of God's people, for the adversary who constantly accused them before God has been 'cast down', i.e. stripped of his power to condemn by Christ's satisfaction of the claims of divine justice on their behalf (Rom. 8:33, 34).

v.11. And they overcame him because of the blood of the Lamb, and because of the word of their testimony; and they loved not their life even unto death.

The victory of Christ's faithful witnesses is so certain that it is spoken of here as though it were already an accomplished fact. They overcame Satan by 'the blood of the Lamb', an evocative phrase which points to the redemptive power of Christ's sacrifice (1:5; 5:9; 7:14). The power of Christ's love for them was also the source of their own fidelity to him, enabling them to remain true to 'the word of their testimony' without regard to the consequences. For they chose to die rather than deny the Lord who bought them with his blood (cf. 6:9; 11:7).

v.12. Therefore rejoice, O heavens, and ye that dwell in them. Woe for the earth and for the sea: because the devil is gone down unto you, having great wrath, knowing that he hath but a short time.

The angel bids the inhabitants of heaven to rejoice in the downfall of the accuser (v. 10), but warns of woe for the earth and sea because the devil has descended in great wrath. He is spurred on by the knowledge that he has only a short time in which to do his evil work (vv. 6, 13, 14). 'The troubles of the persecuted righteous arise not because Satan is too strong, but because he is beaten. He is doing all the harm he can while he can. But he will not be able to do this for much longer' (Morris).

v.13. **And when the dragon saw that he was cast down to the earth, he persecuted the woman that brought forth the man child.**

Having been cast down from heaven (v. 9), it is hardly surprising that the dragon now pursues (in order to persecute, cf. Exod. 14:8; Acts 26:11) the woman whose Son had conquered him. 'If he cannot directly attack the Woman's Son, he can hurt the Son through the Mother (cf. Matt. 25:45; Acts 9:4)' (Swete).

v.14. **And there were given to the woman the two wings of the great eagle, that she might fly into the wilderness unto her place, where she is nourished for a time, and times, and half a time, from the face of the serpent.**

This explains how the woman escaped from the dragon (v. 6), who is here called 'the serpent' because of the flood of lies that pours from his mouth (vv. 9, 15). As God delivered his people from the Egyptians, so the woman was borne on eagle's wings to the safety of the wilderness and nourished with food from heaven (Exod. 19:4; Deut. 32:10, 11). She is thus divinely preserved throughout the period of her trial, which extends from the time of Christ's enthronement (v. 5) until the judgement (so Lenski: see also comment on 11:2).

vv.15, 16. **And the serpent cast out of his mouth after the woman water as a river, that he might cause her to be carried away by** the stream. **And the earth helped the woman, and the earth opened her mouth and swallowed up the river which the dragon cast out of his mouth.**

Although the serpent is unable to follow the woman in her flight, he sends forth a great flood of water to sweep her away, but she is rescued by the earth which swallows up the torrent. The proverbial deceit of the serpent is manifested in a stream of deadly delusions which would engulf the church if they were not providentially diverted. This river of lies is the satanic parody of the river of life which flows from the heavenly throne (21:1).

v.17-13:1. **And the dragon waxed wroth with the woman, and went away to make war with the rest of her seed, that keep the commandments of God, and hold the testimony of Jesus: and he stood upon the sand of the sea.**

The dragon was enraged at the escape of the woman, and went off to make war against the rest of her seed, who are characterized as those 'that keep the commandments of God, and maintain the testimony that Jesus bore' (cf. 1:2; 1 Tim. 6:13). 'If he can neither unseat the Throned Christ nor destroy the Church, yet individual Christians may enjoy no such immunity' (Swete). So the dragon stood by the seashore to summon the beast from the sea to assist him in his fierce campaign of persecution (ch. 13).

Revelation 13

The beast with seven heads and ten horns which rises from the sea is given power by the dragon, and becomes the object of an idolatrous worship (vv. 1-6). He persecutes the saints, and is assisted by the beast that emerges from the earth, which kills all who will not receive the mark of the first beast (vv. 7-18).

v.1b. **And I saw a beast coming up out of the sea, having ten horns and seven heads, and on his horns ten diadems, and upon his heads names of blasphemy.**

At the behest of the dragon (v. 1a), there appeared a terrible beast rising up from the sea, whose chaotic depths are the abode of demonic powers (cf. 11:7; Dan. 7:2-8). The dragon's deputy is like the dragon, for it also has ten horns and seven heads (12:3). It represents the persecuting power of human government, first as manifested in the Roman Empire, and later to be realized in full in the reign of Antichrist. The ten horns with ten diadems symbolize the ten kings who will be the allies of Antichrist in the final conflict (17:12-14). The titles of blasphemy written on the seven heads clearly point to the divine honours assumed by the Roman emperors, which culminated in Domitian's demand that he be addressed as 'our Lord and God'.

v.2. **And the beast which I saw was like unto a leopard, and his feet were as the feet of a bear, and his mouth as the mouth of** a lion: and the dragon gave him his power, and his throne, and great authority.

This beast combined the characteristics of the first three beasts of Daniel 7:4-6 together with the horns of the fourth beast (Dan. 7:7, 8) and was thus the summation of the evil powers manifested in successive world empires. But it was the dragon which gave the beast such power. 'The Dragon works through the Beast as his agent; the war is of Satan's making, but the Empire is his tool for waging it' (Swete).

v.3. **And I saw one of his heads as though it had been smitten unto death; and his death-stroke was healed: and the whole earth wondered after the beast . . .**

In a parody of the death and resurrection of the Lamb (5:6), the mortal wound received by the beast in one of its heads was healed. This probably refers to Nero, whose notoriety as the arch-persecutor of God's people made him the fit symbol of Antichrist, the last incarnation of evil (see the further comments on 17:8-13). Nero's suicide in A.D. 68 seemed to be the death of the beast as a persecuting power. But the fact that this wound was healed shows that the beast's capacity 'to make war with the saints' (v. 7) was soon renewed. Nero's death had been followed by a series of political upheavals which threatened to destroy the empire, but when it was rescued from ruin by Vespasian (A.D. 69-79), the whole world wondered at the recuperative power of the beast. 'The vitality of the pagan empire, shown in this power of righting itself after the revolution, only added to its prestige. The infatuation of loyalty, expressing itself in the worship of the emperor as the personal embodiment of the empire, grew worse and worse' (Moffatt).

v.4. **. . . and they worshipped the dragon, because he gave his authority unto the beast; and they worshipped the beast, saying,**

Who is like unto the beast? and who is able to war with him?

As the authority of the beast came from the dragon, those who worshipped the beast also worshipped the evil power which was behind it. John thus equates the imperial cult with the worship of Satan. The praise given to the beast is a parody of the true worship of God (cf. Exod. 15:11). The second question reflects the crisis facing the churches of Asia Minor when John wrote this book, for Domitian (A.D. 81-96) was the first emperor to demand that his subjects should worship him as 'Lord and God'.

v.5. **And there was given to him a mouth speaking great things and blasphemies; and there was given to him authority to continue forty and two months.**

The blasphemous pretensions of the Roman emperors are only the first stage in the beast's career, which is to continue for 'forty and two months', i.e. throughout the period of the church's witness (cf. Dan. 7:8, 25; see also comment on 11:2). It was the dragon who gave the beast power and authority (vv. 2, 4), but the repeated passive ('was given') indicates that the beast always remains under the control of God (vv. 5, 7). The saints are thus assured that the power of evil is not absolute. For not only has God set a limit upon it, but he will even make it contribute to the final good of his people (Rom. 8:28).

v.6. **And he opened his mouth for blasphemies against God, to blaspheme his name, and his tabernacle, even them that dwell in the heaven.**

The beast opens his mouth to blaspheme against God's name and his tabernacle, which is identified with those 'that dwell in heaven'. This either denotes 'the heavenly host', or the church viewed ideally as seated in heaven (Eph. 2:6). If 'tabernacle' is understood in the light of 21:3, 'The tabernacle of God is with men, and he shall dwell with them', then the phrase will refer to God's faithful people on earth, whose 'citizenship is in heaven' (Phil. 3:20). This means that God regards the persecution of those who bear his name as a blasphemy which is directed against him.

v. 7. **And it was given unto him to make war with the saints, and to overcome them: and there was given to him authority over every tribe and people and tongue and nation.**

The beast was also allowed to make war with the saints and overcome them (Dan. 7:21). He was given the power to persecute and kill the saints, but not to overcome their faith. Thus the beast enjoys only an apparent success; the real victory belongs to the saints who remain faithful unto death (12:11). The four-fold enumeration in the second part of the verse emphasizes the universal authority granted to the beast. 'Wherever the Gospel was carried, Rome was there beforehand; the Beast's authority extended over all the nations and races which surrounded the Mediterranean' (Swete).

v. 8. **And all that dwell on the earth shall worship him, every one whose name hath not been written from the foundation of the world in the book of life of the Lamb that hath been slain.**

'Every one whose name hath not been written in the book of life of the Lamb that hath been slain from the foundation of the world' (ASV margin). All the (unbelieving) inhabitants of the earth will join in the worship of the beast, because their names have not been written in the Lamb's book of life (21:27). The plain inference is that those who are enrolled in that heavenly register will refuse to bow to the beast. Although 17:8 supports the ASV text, it is more natural here to connect 'from the foundation of the world' with 'slain' rather than with 'written', as in the ASV margin cited above. In the eternal purpose of God, Christ is the Lamb who has been slain from the foundation of

the world (1 Peter 1:20). Those whose names are written in the
Lamb's book of life are those for whom he died. Thus election
to eternal life also includes the means of redemption.

vv.9, 10. **If any man hath an ear, let him hear. If any man is for
captivity, into captivity he goeth: if any man shall kill with the
sword, with the sword must he be killed. Here is the patience
and the faith of the saints.**

The repetition of the formula that occurs at the end of each of
the letters to the seven churches here introduces a solemn charge
to the readers (cf. 2:7 etc.). The first couplet points to the
inevitability of the forthcoming test of their fidelity. If any man
is destined for captivity, then he must be willing to accept it in
a spirit of humble submission (cf. Jer. 15:2). The second couplet
warns them against the folly of resorting to force, and recalls the
saying of Jesus: 'All that take the sword shall perish with the
sword' (Matt. 26:52). To meet the persecution inflicted by the
beast in this spirit demonstrates the steadfast endurance and
unwavering faith of the saints.

v.11. **And I saw another beast coming up out of the earth; and
he had two horns like unto a lamb, and he spake as a dragon.**

John next saw arising from the earth another beast, whose harm-
less appearance was betrayed by its roaring voice (Matt. 7:15).
For though it looked like a lamb, it spoke like a dragon. This
beast, which is later called 'the false prophet' (16:13; 19:20;
20:10), represents false religion as the servant of the secular
power. In John's day the beast operated through the priests who
acted as the propagandists of the Caesar-cult by aping a spiritual
power which they did not possess in the interests of a persecuting
state.

v.12. **And he exerciseth all the authority of the first beast in his sight. And he maketh the earth and them that dwell therein to worship the first beast, whose death-stroke was healed.**

The second beast has all the authority of the first beast and exercises it with his approval ('in his sight'). This is because the sole aim of the second beast is to make all men worship the first beast, 'whose death-stroke was healed' (see comment on v. 3). 'The true prophet lives in the presence of God, taking his orders from Him and doing His pleasure; the False Prophet stands before the Beast, whose interpreter and servant he is' (Swete).

v.13. **And he doeth great signs, that he should even make fire to come down out of heaven upon the earth in the sight of men.**

The false prophet authenticates his mission of deceit by means of pseudo-miracles, and in a parody of true spiritual power even makes fire come down from heaven for the admiration of his dupes (Deut. 13:1; 1 Kings 18:38; Matt. 24:24; Rev. 11:5). The trickery of magic was practised by all the religious charlatans of the day, and the apparent miracle of producing fire from heaven was evidently used by the priests of the imperial cult to persuade men to worship the emperor's image (vv. 14, 15).

vv.14, 15. **And he deceiveth them that dwell on the earth by reason of the signs which it was given him to do in the sight of the beast; saying to them that dwell on the earth, that they should make an image to the beast who hath the stroke of the sword and lived. And it was given unto him to give breath to it, even to the image of the beast, that the image of the beast should both speak, and cause that as many as should not worship the image of the beast should be killed.**

The second beast was given the power to deceive 'them that dwell on the earth', i.e. the unbelieving world (cf. 6:10). He instructs the people to make an image of the beast that recovered from the stroke of the sword (v. 3). And he was given the power to animate the idol, which not only spoke, but also demanded the death of all who refused to worship it. In the ancient world statues were regarded as the natural means by which gods could have intercourse with their worshippers and were accredited with the power of working miracles (Charles). There is good reason to believe that the trick of making the statue of the emperor speak was well within the power of the imperial priesthood, for similar ventriloquism was practised by the priests of the oriental cults. ' "Might is right" is the motto of worldliness; "Right is might" is the motto of faith, and those who hold it cannot worship the beast, even though the stroke of his death-wound is healed. Men have appealed to lying miracles on behalf of a death-wounded creed: the cleverness of self-interested partisanship is seldom barren of imposing expedients' (Carpenter).

vv.16, 17. **And he causeth all, the small and the great, and the rich and the poor, and the free and the bond, that there be given them a mark on their right hand, or upon their forehead; and that no man should be able to buy or to sell, save he that hath the mark, even the name of the beast or the number of his name.**

In a parody of the sealing of the redeemed (7:3), the second beast demands that universal allegiance be given to the first beast and forces all to receive the mark of the monster. Although this was a visible mark in the vision, there is no need to imagine that the emperor's worshippers were literally stamped with the number of his name (v. 18). To receive the mark is to partake of the character of the beast, but as believers are identified with a very different image, they would easily be distinguished from the beast's followers. It would seem that the Christians in Smyrna were already subject to economic sanctions because of their faith (2:9). Here the purpose of the boycott is to bring them to the notice of the imperial authorities so that none should escape (Charles).

v.18. **Here is wisdom. He that hath understanding, let him count the number of the beast; for it is the number of a man: and his number is Six hundred and sixty six.**

The announcement, 'Here is wisdom', is followed by the call to the man of understanding to calculate the number of the beast: it is the number of a man and his number is 666. In Hebrew and Greek the letters of the alphabet were used as numerical symbols, so that a name could be equated with the number which consisted of the sum of its letters, e.g. Jesus = 888. It has been shown that when Nero Caesar is rendered into Hebrew it yields the required number 666, and this strongly suggests that the identification first arose among believers who spoke Hebrew or Aramaic (cf. 'Maranatha', 1 Cor. 16:22). John's readers were probably acquainted with this tradition, and the use of such a code would have protected them from further charges of subversion against the state. There is additional significance in the number itself, for each digit of 666 falls short of the perfect number 7. Moreover, the contrast between 666 and 888 shows the gulf which separates the Devil's 'Christ' from God's Christ (see G. R. Beasley-Murray's excellent exposition).

Revelation 14

John sees the Lamb with the 144,000 who have been sealed and hears the song of the redeemed (vv. 1-5). Three angels announce the nearness of the end, the fall of Babylon and the doom of the beast's worshippers (vv. 6-11). The faithful who die in the Lord are promised blessing and rest (vv. 12, 13). Two visions depict the harvest of the earth and the winepress of God's wrath (vv. 14-20).

v.1. And I saw, and behold, the Lamb standing on the mount Zion, and with him a hundred and forty and four thousand, having his name, and the name of his Father, written on their foreheads.

The grim scenes of the previous chapter are now followed by a vision of glorious hope. John saw the victorious Lamb standing on the heavenly Mount Zion with 144,000, a figure which signifies the whole company of the redeemed (see comment on 7:4). This means that all the sealed were saved; not one of the elect was lost. The seal on the foreheads of the chosen is here shown to consist of the name of the Lamb and that of his Father (7:3). 'These two names are the seal because no man comes to the Father save by the Son' (John 14:6).' (Lenski).

v.2. And I heard a voice from heaven, as the voice of many waters, and as the voice of a great thunder: and the voice which I heard was as the voice of harpers harping with their harps . . .

The voice (or sound) which John heard from heaven made such an impression upon him that he uses three similes to describe it. It was like the roar of many waters; it was as loud as a peal of thunder, and its entrancing melody resembled the music made by many harpists. This is the song of redemption which can only be sung by those who have experienced its joys (v. 3).

v.3. . . . and they sing as it were a new song before the throne, and before the four living creatures and the elders: and no man could learn the song save the hundred and forty and four thousand, even they that had been purchased out of the earth.

'As it were a new song.' 'Not actually new, It is the old, old song of redemption which is their theme. But their circumstances are so changed that it is sung with new joy, and through endless ages it will be ever new. Only those can learn this song who are redeemed from the earth. It befits only the Church of God; and not only is their position clearly defined, but their character is definitely given (v. 4)' (Clemance).

v.4. These are they that were not defiled with women; for they are virgins. These are they that follow the Lamb whithersoever he goeth. These were purchased from among men, to be the first-fruits unto God and unto the Lamb.

The virginity of the 144,000 must be understood symbolically of their complete separation from the pollution of idolatry. They kept their spiritual chastity by resisting the seductions of the great harlot (17:2; cf. 2 Cor. 11:2). They are free of impurity because they did not worship the beast and his image (13:15). Such a capitulation to the powers of evil was ruled out by their commitment to Christ. It was their habit on earth to render implicit obedience to the Lamb, for, as the purchase of his passion, they knew themselves to be wholly consecrated to God and to their Saviour. Since the 144,000 are the totality of

the redeemed, 'firstfruits' cannot here mean that there are more
to follow, but carries the more usual sense of an offering to God
(see Charles, Vol. II, p.6).

v.5. **And in their mouth was found no lie: they are without
blemish.**

More is meant than simple honesty, for unlike the pagan world
'which exchanged the truth of God for a lie' (Rom. 1:25), the
144,000 had rejected the deceit of the beast and cast Satan's lie
behind them (21:27; 22:15; cf. John 8:44; 1 John 2:21, 22).
The last thing that John says about the condition of the redeemed
in glory is that they are without blemish and without fault.
'Their being without fault is but the completion of a work which
was going on here; it is a receiving the last finishing touch and
impress of the Spirit's seal. That last impress stamped out the
marks of the last sin' (Clemance).

vv.6, 7. **And I saw another angel flying in mid heaven, having
eternal good tidings to proclaim unto them that dwell on the earth,
and unto every nation and tribe and tongue and people; and he
saith with a great voice, Fear God, and give him glory; for the
hour of his judgement is come: and worship him that made the
heaven and the earth and sea and fountains of waters.**

After this anticipation of the bliss of the redeemed (vv. 1-5),
three angels appear to warn of the approaching judgement
(vv. 6-11). It is important to realize that John saw a series
of visions which were intended to convey an intelligible message
that was permanently valid. Hence it is a mistake to become pre-
occupied with the bizarre details of the visions to the detriment
of the clear declarations they contain. There is no need for any
angel to fly in mid-heaven at some future date, for the warning
thus conveyed to the world through John holds good to the end
of the age. In contrast to the beast's empty claim to universal

dominion, the everlasting sovereignty of the Creator of the world is indeed 'eternal good tidings' to those with reverent and submissive hearts. The angelic summons is not a preaching of *the* gospel (the Greek lacks the article), but is a call to the earth's inhabitants to awake to the reality of God's rule before it is too late (cf. Acts 14:15).

v.8. And another, a second angel, followed, saying, Fallen, fallen, is Babylon the great, that hath made all the nations to drink of the wine of the wrath of her fornication.

The second angel announces the fall of Babylon (Jer. 51:7). The image is a fit symbol of human society organized against God, and to the early Christians new Rome was but old Babylon writ large (1 Peter 5:13). Here the prophetic past tense points to the certainty of the judgement which is vividly portrayed in chapter 18. Two ideas are combined in the phrase, 'the wine of the wrath of her fornication'. Babylon is represented as the great harlot who intoxicates the nations with the wine of her fornication (17:2, 4, 6), but God will punish these infidelities by making her drain the cup of his wrath (v. 10; 16:19; cf. Jer. 25:15).

vv.9,10. And another angel, a third, followed them, saying with a great voice, If any man worshippeth the beast and his image, and receiveth a mark on his forehead, or upon his hand, he also shall drink of the wine of the wrath of God, which is prepared unmixed in the cup of his anger; and he shall be tormented with fire and brimstone in the presence of the holy angels, and in the presence of the Lamb . . .

The third angel warns of the terrible punishment which will befall any man who worships the beast and receives his mark. He shall drink of the wine of God's wrath, which is 'mingled unmixed' (ASV margin) in the cup of his anger. The first word of this paradoxical phrase refers to the ancient practice of mixing wine with spices to make it more powerful; the second word means that its strength is not diluted by the addition of water. To drink the cup of God's wrath involves being tormented with fire and brimstone in the presence of the holy angels and of the Lamb (19:20; 20:10; 21:8). This suggests that the most poignant factor in the pain of the wicked will be to see 'the triumph of the Lamb, against whom as worshippers of the Beast they had made war' (Beckwith).

v.11. . . . **and the smoke of their torment goeth up for ever and ever; and they have no rest day and night, they that worship the beast and his image, and whoso receiveth the mark of his name.**

The phrase 'for ever and ever' is predicated of God in 4:9, and this means that the torment of the beast's followers is as endless as God himself (Anthony Hoekema). Had John wished to convey the impression that the punishment of the wicked was only of limited duration, he could hardly have chosen a more misleading phrase to describe it! However, their punishment is endless because their guilt is endless. 'The demand that penal suffering shall stop when it has once begun, is as irrational as the demand that guilt shall stop when it has once begun. The *continuous* nature of guilt necessitates the endlessness of retribution' (Shedd, *Dogmatic Theology,* Vol. II, p.722).

v.12. **Here is the patience of the saints, they that keep the commandments of God, and the faith of Jesus.**

Since such a judgement will overtake the worshippers of the beast, John issues a call to the saints to exhibit that patient endurance which consists in keeping the commandments of God and trusting in Jesus. Those with a living faith in Jesus would rather die than be disloyal to their Lord. 'The Caesar-cult supplied the Saints with a test of loyalty which strengthened and matured those who were worthy of the name' (Swete).

v.13. **And I heard a voice from heaven saying, Write, Blessed are the dead who die in the Lord from henceforth: yea, saith the Spirit, that they may rest from their labours; for their works follow with them.**

John then heard a voice from heaven instructing him to write down an important message which promises blessedness to all who die in the Lord 'from henceforth'. This final phrase does not deny the same blessedness to saints who died previously, but is added to bring special comfort to those who would soon be required to seal their testimony with their blood. But though the message is here applied to the particular crisis that faced the church of John's day, the assurance thus given belongs to believers in every age. This promise is confirmed and further explained by an emphatic utterance of the Spirit. For the blessedness of those who die in union with the Lord consists not only in rest from their exhausting toil, but also in the enjoyment of their works of faith which follow them to heaven (2:2). No labour for the Lord is ever lost (1 Cor. 15:58).

v.14. **And I saw, and behold, a white cloud; and on the cloud I saw one sitting like unto a son of man, having on his head a golden crown, and in his hand a sharp sickle.**

John next saw the advent in judgement of one 'like unto a son of man', sitting on a white cloud and wearing a golden crown (Dan. 7:13). This description could apply to no one but Christ. He is holding a sharp sickle in readiness to reap the harvest of the earth (v. 15). As the harvest is the end of the world, that which is reaped should not be restricted to the righteous only. 'The figure is comprehensive, including in a word the whole process of the winding up of the ages, and the recompense of both the good and the bad' (Beckwith).

vv.15, 16. **And another angel came out from the temple, crying with a great voice to him that sat on the cloud, Send forth thy sickle, and reap: for the hour to reap is come; for the harvest of the earth is ripe. And he that sat on the cloud cast his sickle upon the earth; and the earth was reaped.**

Some have felt it inappropriate that an angel should convey a command to Christ, but this objection overlooks the fact that the angel is sent from the temple by God. 'The angel acts as the messenger of the will of God to Christ in his capacity as Son of man, because the command is one concerning the times and seasons which the Father hath kept in his own power' (Plummer). It is remarkable that mere men should still presume to predict the time of the end when even Christ cannot reap the harvest of the earth until the moment determined by God (Mark 13:32; Acts 1:7).

v.17. **And another angel came out from the temple which is in heaven, he also having a sharp sickle.**

The general picture of the last judgement given in the previous vision is now followed by a gruesome close-up of the effect of God's vengeance upon the wicked (vv. 17-20). The appearance of another angel from the heavenly temple is significant, for it shows that he is the agent of God's judgement. He also wields a sharp sickle for his task of reaping the vintage of the earth (Joel 3:13).

v.18. **And another angel came out from the altar, he that hath power over fire; and he called with a great voice to him that had the sharp sickle, saying, Send forth thy sharp sickle, and gather the clusters of the vine of the earth; for her grapes are fully ripe.**

There now appears on the scene yet another angel. This one comes from the altar and has power over fire, which presumably means the fire of judgement. 'He comes from the altar, upon which was offered the incense accompanying the prayers of the saints for judgement' (Beckwith). It is in response to those prayers that he instructs the angel with the sharp sickle to cut down the clusters from the vine of the earth, for its grapes are at last fully ripe for judgement (cf. 6:9; 8:3).

v.19. **And the angel cast his sickle into the earth, and gathered the vintage of the earth, and cast it into the winepress, the great winepress, of the wrath of God.**

The angel at once obeyed and gathered the vintage of the earth, and cast it into the great winepress of God's wrath. Here the primitive method of treading the grapes to extract their juice becomes a graphic symbol of the fierceness of the divine anger (19:15; cf. Isa. 63:3).

v.20. **And the winepress was trodden without the city, and there came out blood from the winepress, even unto the bridles of the horses, as far as a thousand and six hundred furlongs.**

The judgement is depicted as taking place 'without the city', which probably refers to the exclusion of the wicked from the society of the redeemed (cf. 20:9). The universality of the judgement is indicated by a ghastly image. The red juice of the grape pours from an ordinary winepress, but a sea of blood flows from this winepress, and reaches as high as the bridles of horses and extends as far as 1600 stadia. The number is again symbolic, and is derived from the square of 4 (the number of the earth, 7:1) multiplied by the square of 10 (the number of completeness). It thus signifies 'completeness as regards the created world, and the inability of anyone to escape God's judgement' (Plummer).

Section 5

The seven bowls of wrath

Revelation 15

After a vision of seven angels holding the last seven plagues, John saw those who had overcome the beast singing the song of Moses and of the Lamb (vv. 1-4). The seven angels then came forth from the heavenly temple with the seven bowls of God's wrath (vv. 5-8).

v.1. And I saw another sign in heaven, great and marvellous, seven angels having seven plagues, which are the last, for in them is finished the wrath of God.

As the previous chapter closed with another account of the end, it is evident that the events portrayed in these visions are not presented in chronological order. Hence it seems best to regard the cycles of judgement represented by the seals, the trumpets and the bowls as covering the same period in history from three different viewpoints. This verse stands as the frontispiece to what follows, for John introduces the seven angels as if they were all present at one moment, when in fact he sees their actions in succession. The entire vision (chs 15, 16) is a great and marvellous portent because the wrath of God reaches its goal in the end-time judgements which are symbolized by these last seven plagues.

v.2. And I saw as it were a sea of glass mingled with fire; and them that come off victorious from the beast, and from his image, and from the number of his name, standing by the sea of glass, having harps of God.

John first saw what looked like 'a sea of glass' in 4:6, where it represents God's transcendence, but here it is 'mingled with fire', to show that God's wrath is about to fall upon the persecutors of his saints (cf. 8:5). The conquerors of the beast are those who have not worshipped his image nor received as a mark the number of his name (13:14-18). Having safely emerged from their time of trial, they now stand on the crystal pavement of heaven, holding harps to accompany their hymn of grateful praise to God (vv. 3, 4).

vv.3, 4. **And they sing the song of Moses the servant of God, and the song of the Lamb, saying, Great and marvellous are thy works, O Lord God, the Almighty; righteous and true are thy ways, thou King of the ages. Who shall not fear, O Lord, and glorify thy name? For thou only art holy; for all the nations shall come and worship before thee; for thy righteous acts have been made manifest.**

Although they sing one song of praise to God, it is called the song of Moses and the song of the Lamb, because the deliverance God wrought through his servant Moses foreshadowed that which he wrought through the Lamb. The continuity of God's saving purpose in both dispensations means that the Old Testament phrases which make up the hymn can be applied to the greater exodus which he accomplished through Christ (cf. Exod. 15:1-18). Verse 3 celebrates the great and marvellous works of Almighty God; all his ways are righteous and true, as befits the King whose sovereignty spans the ages (Ps. 139:14; Amos 4:13; Deut. 32:4; Jer. 10:10). The challenge of verse 4, 'Who shall not fear, O Lord, and glorify thy name?' (cf. Jer. 10:7), is followed by three clauses giving the reasons for paying this tribute of praise to God.
1.	God is the Holy One, who is unapproachably great (Ps. 99:3).
2.	His universal dominion must lead to universal homage (Ps. 86:9).
3.	The righteousness of his judicial sentences is now manifest to all (Ps. 98:2). 'The teaching of Scripture is that in the end the

whole universe shall acknowledge the righteousness of all God's acts and verdicts' (Lenski).

vv.5, 6. **And after these things I saw, and the temple of the tabernacle of the testimony in heaven was opened: and there came out from the temple the seven angels that had the seven plagues, arrayed with precious stone, pure and bright, and girt about their breasts with golden girdles.**

After hearing this song (vv. 3, 4), John saw the heavenly temple opened and there came out the seven angels with the seven plagues. Here the temple is called 'the tabernacle of the testimony' (Exod. 38:21), because that tent 'contained the ark with the law of God which testifies against sin' (Marvin Vincent). As nothing but sin calls forth God's wrath, his punitive judgements must be recognized as the just recompense of man's sinfulness. The celestial purity of these angels is indicated by their dress. They were clothed in 'pure bright linen, and their breasts girded with golden girdles' (RSV). The ASV follows the harder reading advocated by Westcott and Hort, but 'stone' makes no sense here and must be rejected as a transcriptional error (see Bruce M. Metzger, *A Textual Commentary on the Greek New Testament,* p.756).

v. 7. **And one of the four living creatures gave unto the seven angels seven golden bowls full of the wrath of God, who liveth for ever and ever.**

One of the angelic throne-attendants (see comment on 4:6) acts as an intermediary in giving the avenging angels the seven bowls which were full of the wrath of God (Robert Mounce). The fact that God 'liveth for ever and ever' means that his promised judgements are no idle threats, but a dreadful reality which the wicked will soon experience in full measure.

v.8. **And the temple was filled with smoke from the glory of God, and from his power; and none was able to enter into the temple, till the seven plagues of the seven angels should be finished.**

The smoke that filled the temple was the symbol of the glory and power of God (Exod. 40:34; Isa. 6:4). It was also the sign of the imminence of his judgements. 'Smouldering fires of indignation are now on the point of bursting into punishment from the arsenal of anger. Hence, till the plagues are over, God's presence is unendurable' (Moffatt).

Revelation 16

The seven angels are commanded to empty the bowls of God's wrath upon the earth, and the plagues which follow reach their climax in the destruction of Babylon (vv. 1-21).

v.1. And I heard a great voice out of the temple, saying to the seven angels, Go ye, and pour out the seven bowls of the wrath of God into the earth.

As no one could enter the temple until the seven plagues were finished (15:8), it would seem that the great voice John heard from the temple was that of God himself. Although the angels have received the seven bowls of wrath (15:7), they must await the command of God before they can pour them out. The contents of the bowls are very similar to the woes announced by the trumpets. The plagues in both series recall those that fell upon Egypt before the exodus, and cover the same period in history terminating with the last judgement day.

v.2. And the first went, and poured out his bowl into the earth; and it became a noisome and grievous sore upon the men that had the mark of the beast, and that worshipped his image.

The first plague of foul and malignant sores is like the Egyptian plague of boils (Exod. 9:9-11), and is a fitting punishment for those who had received the mark of the beast. 'The victims of the scourge are declared to be the worshippers of the Beast; that this is true of the other plagues is clear, though not expressly stated' (Beckwith).

vv.3, 4. **And the second poured out his bowl into the sea; and it became blood as of a dead man; and every living soul died, even the things that were in the sea. And the third poured out his bowl into the rivers and the fountains of the waters; and it became blood.**

The second plague turns the sea into blood and destroys all marine life, while the third also turns the sources of fresh water into blood (Exod. 7:17-21). The judgement of the second and third bowls is total, whereas that of the second and third trumpets was only partial (cf. 8:8-11).

vv.5, 6. **And I heard the angel of the waters saying, Righteous art thou, who art and who wast, thou Holy One, because thou didst thus judge: for they poured out the blood of saints and prophets, and blood hast thou given them to drink: they are worthy.**

John next heard the angel in charge of the waters acknowledge the righteousness of God's judgement in turning them into blood. 'The spirit of the waters is so far from resenting the plague that he bears witness to the justice which inflicts it' (Swete). It is because God is righteous, eternal and holy that he has made the punishment fit the crime (on the omission of 'who is to come', see comment on 11:17). As the worshippers of the beast poured out the blood of saints and prophets, so God has given them blood to drink. 'They are worthy' means 'They have their desserts!' (NEB).

v.7. **And I heard the altar saying, Yea, O Lord God, the Almighty, true and righteous are thy judgements.**

The altar is here said to speak because it is associated with the martyrs' plea for vindication in 6:9. 'The altar beneath which the souls of the martyrs cried, and on which the prayers of saints were offered, is represented as confirming the testimony to the just dealings of God' (Carpenter).

vv.8, 9. **And the fourth poured out his bowl upon the sun; and it was given unto it to scorch men with fire. And men were scorched with great heat: and they blasphemed the name of God who hath the power over these plagues; and they repented not to give him glory.**

Whereas the fourth trumpet had reduced the power of the sun by a third (8:12), the fourth bowl so increased its intensity that men were scorched with the excessive heat. But though they clearly saw the hand of God in this and the other plagues, they not only refused to repent but were further hardened and blasphemed the name of God. 'The members of the kingdom of evil are characterized by willing, wilful, and intense hatred of God and holiness, and by an impenitent and blaspheming spirit' (Shedd).

vv.10, 11. **And the fifth poured out his bowl upon the throne of the beast; and his kingdom was darkened; and they gnawed their tongues for pain, and they blasphemed the God of heaven because of their pains and their sores; and they repented not of their works.**

As the fifth plague is poured out upon the throne of the beast, his kingdom is plunged into darkness and his subjects gnaw their tongues in pain (Exod. 10:21-23). They have preferred darkness to light, and now that dreadful choice is confirmed as the darkness of God's anger overwhelms them with anguish. But far from confessing their guilt, they cursed the God of heaven for their spiritual and physical torments, and would not repent of their works. Now where there is no acknowledgement of God's justice, there can be no experience of his mercy. 'Accordingly, in all the Biblical descriptions of the lost, the absence of sorrow for sin as related to justice, and the hatred of justice itself, are invariable elements. Satan and his angels, together with condemned men, are utterly and malignantly impenitent' (Shedd).

v.12. **And the sixth poured out his bowl upon the great river, the river Euphrates; and the water thereof was dried up, that the way might be made ready for the kings that come from the sun-rising.**

The sixth bowl prepares the way for the final conflict by drying up the river Euphrates to allow the kings from the east (literally, 'from the sunrising') to advance on Rome (Babylon). This apparently alludes to the contemporary belief that a revived Nero would return from the east with the dreaded Parthian hordes to ravage the empire. What follows shows that Nero will indeed return — not literally, but in the shape of that persecuting ruler who will be the last opponent of the people of God (see comments on 17:8-11). Here the kings from the east represent the Parthian provincial governors, who are probably to be identified with the ten kings of 17:12, 13.

vv.13, 14. **And I saw coming out of the mouth of the dragon, and out of the mouth of the beast, and out of the mouth of the false prophet, three unclean spirits, as it were frogs: for they are spirits of demons, working signs; which go forth unto the kings of the whole world, to gather them together unto the war of the great day of God, the Almighty.**

John sees three unclean spirits that look like frogs coming out of the mouths of the dragon (Satan, 12:3), the beast (world power, 13:1) and the false prophet (false religion, 13:11). The fact that these demonic spirits proceed from the *mouths* of this unholy trinity indicates the nature of their task. As the lying spirit enticed Ahab into battle (1 Kings 22:21-23), so they are sent forth with deceitful words and signs to persuade the kings of the world to join in the great final battle (cf. 19:11-21). But though the unclean spirits thus gather the world rulers against the Lord and his anointed (Ps. 2:2), they fail to understand that their preparations only pave the way for 'the great day of God, the Almighty'.

v.15. **(Behold, I come as a thief. Blessed is he that watcheth, and keepeth his garments, lest he walk naked, and they see his shame.)**

It is entirely appropriate that Christ should interject a warning at this point concerning the unexpectedness of his coming (3:3; Matt. 24:43; 2 Peter 3:10). 'Blessed are they who are ready, watching. But vigilance is not enough: the garments must be kept. The powers of evil are abroad. Sloth and pleasure may counsel ease, and tempt the watcher to lay aside his garments and take rest and sleep. The earnest watcher desires, like Paul, to be found in Christ, clad in the true righteousness of faith (Phil. 3:9)' (Carpenter). (Cf. 3:18.)

v.16. **And they gathered them together into the place which is called in Hebrew Har-Magedon.**

The unclean spirits fulfilled their mission by gathering the kings together at Har-Magedon. The fact that no translation of the Hebrew word is supplied should alert us to its symbolic significance. The word means 'Mountain of Megiddo', and this presents a serious difficulty as there is no mountain on the plain of Megiddo. Beckwith suggests that 'mountain' may have been drawn from Ezekiel 38:8-21; 39:2, 4, 17, where the last battle takes place on 'the mountains of Israel', and then 'Megiddo' was added because of its fame as the place where Jehovah's enemies perished (Judges 5:19, 31). Hence the name represents an *event* rather than a recognizable geographical *location*.

Har-Magedon is then 'an imaginary name for designating the scene of the great battle between Antichrist and the Messiah' (Beckwith). (Cf. 19:11-21.)

v.17. **And the seventh poured out his bowl upon the air; and there came forth a great voice out of the temple, from the throne, saying, It is done . . .**

The pouring out of the seventh bowl upon the air is followed by a storm and an earthquake of unexampled severity (v. 18). The voice of God is again heard coming from the throne of the temple, saying, 'It is done' (v. 1). The declaration marks the end of God's judgements and the accomplishment of his purpose.

v.18. **. . . and there were lightnings, and voices, and thunders; and there was a great earthquake, such as was not since there were men upon the earth, so great an earthquake, so mighty.**

The appalling portents of God's wrath in the sky are accompanied by the most devastating earthquake the world has ever known. 'Writing in a century remarkable for the number and severity of its earthquakes, and to men whose country was specially subject to them, St John is careful to distinguish this final shock from even the greatest hitherto known' (Swete).

v.19. **And the great city was divided into three parts, and the cities of the nations fell: and Babylon the great was remembered in the sight of God, to give unto her the cup of the wine of the fierceness of his wrath.**

The earthquake brought about the complete disintegration of the great city ('split into three'), and it also destroyed the cities of the nations, thus bringing antichristian civilization to an end. It is because the great city of Babylon (Rome) made the whole earth drunk with 'the wine of her fornication' (17:2) that she is now made to drink 'the wine of the fierceness of his wrath'. God appeared to have forgotten the great city during the time that she filled up the cup of her iniquities, but when judgement strikes at last, it becomes clear that God has not forgotten her offences.

v.20. **And every island fled away, and the mountains were not found.**

The completeness of the destruction is indicated by the disappearance of every island and mountain. 'No city, even on the most remote island, no fortress of the antichristian empire on a single mountain height escaped the destructive final wrath' (Lenski).

v.21. **And great hail, every stone about the weight of a talent, cometh down out of heaven upon men: and men blasphemed God because of the plague of the hail; for the plague thereof is exceeding great.**

The dreadful effusion of God's wrath reaches its climax in a plague of hailstones so huge that they weighed about a hundred pounds each. Yet even this terrible visitation fails to move the wicked to repentance. 'Even Pharaoh had shown signs of repentance under the hail (Exod. 9:27), though he relapsed into impenitence as soon as it had ceased; but the age of the last plague blasphemed while it suffered' (Swete).

Section 6
The fall of Babylon

Revelation 17

John is first shown the harlot, Babylon the great, who is drunk with the blood of the saints (vv. 1-6). The angel then explains that the woman represents Rome, and that the beast and his allies will act as the instrument of God in destroying the wicked city (vv. 7-18).

v.1. **And there came one of the seven angels that had the seven bowls, and spake with me, saying, Come hither, I will show thee the judgement of the great harlot that sitteth upon many waters ...**

One of the seven angels calls John to see the judgement of the great harlot. She is clearly a parody of the bride whom the same angel will later show to John (21:9). As the apotheosis of worldly influence, she is aptly called Babylon the great, but she represents Rome because the mantle of Babylon's iniquities has now fallen upon that city. Since she is the harlot and not the spouse, her sin is not described as adultery but as fornication. This means that she turns people away from God and lures them into idolatry and immorality (vv. 4, 5). She is depicted as sitting upon many waters, for Babylon was irrigated by an elaborate system of canals (Jer. 51:13). But as applied to Rome, these waters represent the many peoples who are subject to her evil influence (v. 15).

v.2. **... with whom the kings of the earth committed fornication,**

and they that dwell in the earth were made drunken with the wine of her fornication.

Rome is the great harlot 'with whom the kings of the earth committed fornication'. The fornication 'of which these kings were guilty consisted in purchasing the favour of Rome by accepting her suzerainty and with it her vices and idolatries' (Swete). Thus Rome was the metropolis of corruption, who had made the inhabitants of the earth drunk with the wine of her fornication (14:8).

v.3. **And he carried me away in the Spirit into a wilderness: and I saw a woman sitting upon a scarlet-coloured beast, full of names of blasphemy, having seven heads and ten horns.**

The angel then carried John away in the Spirit (1:10) into a wilderness, where he saw a woman sitting on a fearsome beast, for her powers of seduction rest upon the might of the Roman empire (cf. 13:1). The beast is richly draped in scarlet, to indicate the ostentatious magnificence of that empire, and it is covered with the blasphemous claims to deity made by its emperors. The meaning of its seven heads and ten horns is later explained by the angel (vv. 9-14, 16, 17).

v.4. **And the woman was arrayed in purple and scarlet, and decked with gold and precious stone and pearls, having in her hand a golden cup full of abominations, even the unclean things of her fornication . . .**

The woman is arrayed in costly garments and adorned with gold and precious jewels, but the golden cup she holds is full of the abominations of her fornication (21:27; cf. Jer. 51:7). Although she appears to offer a satisfying drink, the golden cup is filled with the 'abominations' of idolatry, which she promotes by her spiritual 'fornication' (cf. Mark 13:14). 'Rome is pronounced luxurious, licentious, and loathsome' (Moffatt).

v.5. . . . **and upon her forehead a name written, Mystery, Babylon the Great, The Mother of the Harlots and of the Abominations of the Earth.**

'And written on her forehead was a name with a secret meaning: "Babylon the great, the mother of whores and of every obscenity on earth" ' (NEB). It was the custom for Roman prostitutes to wear a headband which displayed their names. The word 'mystery' is not part of the name, but warns the reader that the name must be interpreted spiritually (11:8). John calls the woman Babylon, but the initiated will realize that he is in fact referring to Rome. The mother city is here 'viewed as the source and furtherer of all the abominations of the earth' (Beckwith).

v.6. **And I saw the woman drunken with the blood of the saints, and with the blood of the martyrs of Jesus. And when I saw her, I wondered with a great wonder.**

'With the blood of the saints, and with the blood of the witnesses of Jesus' (ASV margin). The capital charge against this woman is that she is a murderess. She kills those who refuse to participate in her abominable idolatries. Her victims are doubly defined as 'the saints' and 'the witnesses of Jesus' — they belong to God, and had borne testimony to Jesus. Probably the primary reference is to those who were martyred at Rome by Nero. Thus the woman not only makes others drunk with the wine of her fornication (v. 2), but she is herself drunk with the blood of God's people (Caird). Having expected to see the judgement of the great harlot (v. 1), John is astonished to be shown a vision in which she glories and triumphs in her sin.

v.7. **And the angel said unto me, Wherefore didst thou wonder?**

I will tell thee the mystery of the woman, and of the beast that carrieth her, which hath the seven heads and the ten horns.

John's amazement at the harlot's apparent success is rebuked by the angel, who proceeds to interpret the mystery of the woman and of·the beast which carries her.

v.8. **The beast that thou sawest was, and is not: and is about to come up out of the abyss, and to go into perdition. And they that dwell on the earth shall wonder, they whose name hath not been written in the book of life from the foundation of the world, when they behold the beast, how that he was, and is not, and shall come.**

The angel first reveals the fate of the beast and thus exposes the emptiness of its divine pretensions. In contrast to the One '*who is* and who was and who is to come' (1:4), the beast John saw 'was, and *is not,* and is about to come up', which is but a feeble parody of the divine title. The career of the beast also parodies that of the Lamb. For the Lamb descends from heaven and returns to heaven, whereas the beast ascends from the abyss only to sink back into perdition (19:20). It is clear from what follows that the beast is to be identified with Nero, who symbolizes the future Antichrist (see also comments on 13:1, 3). Nero committed suicide in A.D. 68, but for twenty years after his death many believed that he had gone to the east and would return at the head of a Parthian army. When this expectation was no longer credible, it was replaced by the still stranger myth that Nero would return from the dead to regain his lost power. At the time of John's vision the Neronic persecution was in the past ('was'), and it would seem from 2:13 that Antipas was the only contemporary martyr ('and is not'), but a revival of the beast's power is now imminent in the renewal of emperor worship by Domitian ('and is about to come up out of the abyss'). But the primary application of the vision to the church of John's day does not rule out its secondary fulfilment in the last days before Christ's return. The beast's supernatural powers will excite the wonder and worship of the unbelieving world. 'True, he *goes to perdition* eventually, but not before all except the elect have succumbed to the fascination of his second advent' (Moffatt).

***vv.9-11*. Here is the mind that hath wisdom. The seven heads are seven mountains, on which the woman sitteth: and they are seven kings; the five are fallen, the one is, the other is not yet come; and when he cometh, he must continue a little while. And the beast that was, and is not, is himself also an eighth, and is of the seven; and he goeth into perdition.**

This difficult passage is prefaced by the warning that spiritual discernment is required in order to understand the mystery of the beast (13:18). A double interpretation is given of the beast's seven heads. They are first said to be the seven mountains on which the woman sits, an unmistakable reference to Rome which no one could fail to recognize, and they are also seven kings representing the full series of Roman emperors. The point of interest lies not in the imperial line which has nearly run its course, but in the coming of an eighth who is also one of the seven. 'The Roman empire must fill out its destined place in history, it must have its complete tale of kings denoted by the typical number seven; then Antichrist comes, who succeeds the Roman power which he destroys; he forms an eighth ruler added to the seventh . . . but at the same time he is "of the seven", inasmuch as he is one of the seven (Nero) reincarnate' (Beckwith).

***vv.12, 13*. And the ten horns that thou sawest are ten kings, who have received no kingdom as yet; but they receive authority as kings, with the beast, for one hour. These have one mind, and they give their power and authority unto the beast.**

The angel further explains that the ten horns John saw are ten kings who have received no kingdom as yet, but they will receive their kingly authority with the beast and will reign with him 'for one hour', i.e. a very short time. They are united in consenting to give their power and authority to the beast, because God put it into their hearts to do this until his words were accomplished (v. 17). These willing allies of the beast are probably the kings from the east mentioned in the previous section (see comment on 16:12).

v.14. **These shall war against the Lamb, and the Lamb shall over-come them, for he is Lord of lords, and King of kings; and they also shall overcome that are with him, called and chosen and faithful.**

This brief preview of the last battle shows that the allies of the beast shall war against the Lamb (19:11-21). Initially this means they will attack the Lamb's followers, but their martyrdom amounts to a victory (13:7), because they have refused to deny their Lord even in the midst of this final onslaught by the powers of evil (12:11). But when the Lamb suddenly appears from heaven he will overcome all his enemies, for he is Lord of lords and King of kings (19:16). The saints with the Lamb will share in his victory as they are 'called and chosen and faithful'. They were effectually called by grace because they were first chosen, and so they have remained faithful (2:10, 13).

v.15. **And he saith unto me, The waters which thou sawest, where the harlot sitteth, are peoples, and multitudes, and nations, and tongues.**

The angel next identifies the waters upon which the harlot sits as the multitudes who are subjected to her corrupting influence (v. 1). Rome was the centre of a civilization which had become drunk 'with the wine of her fornication' (v. 2). Yet Rome's 'greatest danger lay in the multitudes which were under her sway, and out of which would arise the "ten kings" who were to bring about her downfall' (Swete).

v.16. **And the ten horns which thou sawest, and the beast, these shall hate the harlot, and shall make her desolate and naked, and shall eat her flesh, and shall burn her utterly with fire.**

Here the angel reveals the fate of Rome in language that recalls the judgement of the harlot city of Jerusalem (Ezek. 23:25-30). It is because evil contains the seeds of its own destruction that the beast and the ten kings will turn in hatred upon the harlot and completely destroy her. 'Wicked men are not just one happy band of brothers. Being wicked, they give way to jealousy and hatred. At the climax their mutual hatreds will result in mutual destruction' (Morris).

v.17. **For God did put in their hearts to do his mind, and to come to one mind, and to give their kingdom unto the beast, until the words of God should be accomplished.**

Since this is such a surprising development, the angel explains that the unanimity of the ten kings was no accident, for God moved them to put their power at the disposal of the beast until all God's words were fulfilled. A sovereign God leaves no room for any form of dualism. 'A divine overruling controls all political movements (cf. 11:2; 13:5, 7) . . . The irony of the situation is that the tools of providence are destroyed, after they have unconsciously served their purpose (as in Isa. 10:12f.)' (Moffatt).

v.18. **And the woman whom thou sawest is the great city, which reigneth over the kings of the earth.**

This puts the identity of the woman beyond all doubt. The great harlot is Rome, which rules over the kings of the earth. But

Babylon the great represents more than first-century Rome; it also stands for the final Babylon which is yet to be overthrown (so Mounce).

Revelation 18

A glorious angel proclaims the fall of Babylon (vv. 1-3). God's people are called out before the judgement falls upon her (vv. 4-8). There is great lamentation on earth and rejoicing in heaven (vv. 9-20). Her total destruction is signified by the casting of a great millstone into the sea (vv. 21-24).

v.1. After these things I saw another angel coming down out of heaven, having great authority; and the earth was lightened with his glory.

After the interpreting angel had done his work, John saw another angel coming down from heaven with the divine authority to announce the doom of Babylon. 'So recently has he come from the Presence that in passing he flings a broad belt of light across the dark earth' (Swete). (Cf. Ezek. 43:2.)

v.2. And he cried with a mighty voice, saying, Fallen, fallen is Babylon the great, and is become a habitation of demons, and a hold of every unclean spirit, and a hold of every unclean and hateful bird.

The dramatic declaration, 'Fallen, fallen is Babylon the great,' transfers to the past what is still future, to denote the certainty of the event (Isa. 21:9). The once proud city is viewed as having already become 'a dwelling for demons, a haunt for every unclean

spirit, for every vile and loathsome bird' (NEB). This prophetic
picture presents a scene of utter desolation and degradation.
Deserted of human inhabitants, Babylon is now the dwelling-
place of demons, and the haunt of every unclean spirit and bird
(Isa. 13:19-22; 34:11; Jer. 50:39).

v.3. **For by the wine of the wrath of her fornication all the
nations are fallen; and the kings of the earth committed fornication with her, and the merchants of the earth waxed rich by
the power of her wantonness.**

'For all nations have drunk deep of the fierce wine of her fornication' (NEB). Babylon is so judged because she has intoxicated
the nations with the wine of her fornication (Jer. 51:7). The
kings of the earth have shared in her idolatries and its merchants
have grown rich from the power of her wanton luxury. 'The
history of human civilization is to a great extent the history of
human luxury; and the history of human luxury is the history of
bodily appetites growing more and more inordinate, and growing
by what they feed upon' (W. G. T. Shedd, 'Christian Moderation'
in *Sermons to the Spiritual Man,* p.25). (Cf. 3:17.)

vv.4,5. **And I heard another voice from heaven, saying, Come
forth, my people, out of her, that ye have no fellowship with
her sins, and that ye receive not of her plagues: for her sins have
reached even unto heaven, and God hath remembered her
iniquities.**

The voice John heard from heaven must be that of an angel who
speaks on God's behalf, for the placing of God in the third person
in verse 5 clearly shows that God is not the speaker. The call to
God's people to come out from Babylon does not require local
removal from the place itself (1 Cor. 5:10), but is rather a
demand to the churches for complete moral separation from her
iniquities so that they do not participate in her plagues (Isa. 51:11;

Jer. 51:45; 2 Cor. 6:17). 'The constant danger confronting God's people is to be taken in by the antichristian seduction which seeks to entice and entangle them' (Lenski). The angel further declares that Babylon's sins have been heaped up to heaven like a latter-day tower of Babel, thus forcibly reminding God that the time for judgement has come (Gen. 11:4; Jer. 51:9).

v.6. **Render unto her even as she rendered, and double unto her the double according to her works: in the cup which she mingled, mingle unto her double.**

This command is not addressed to believers, but to the angelic ministers of the divine vengeance (Rom. 12:19). They are instructed to give back the double punishment Babylon deserves for her double sin (Jer. 16:18; 17:18). 'The "double" must not be taken to mean double her sins; her sins are themselves called double, and her judgement is according to her sins. She is double-stained in wickedness, and "the law of retribution fiercely works" in her. The cup of her luxuriousness becomes the cup of vengeance' (Carpenter).

vv. 7, 8. **How much soever she glorified herself, and waxed wanton, so much give her of torment and mourning: for she saith in her heart, I sit a queen, and am no widow, and shall in no wise see mourning. Therefore in one day shall her plagues come, death, and mourning, and famine; and she shall be utterly burned with fire; for strong is the Lord God who judged her.**

The punishment of Babylon will be in direct proportion to her self-glorification and sinful extravagance (Isa. 47:7-9). As she thought no disaster could ever interrupt her reign of pleasure, her plagues will come in a single day, for the strong city (v. 10) is no match for the strong God who judges her (John Sweet). 'The "plagues" of Babylon, when they come, will make a dire antithesis to her present condition; death, mourning, dearth will reign where life at its gayest and fullest has long prevailed. Fire will complete the work of destruction' (Swete).

vv.9, 10. **And the kings of the earth, who committed fornication and lived wantonly with her, shall weep and wail over her, when they look upon the smoke of her burning, standing afar off for the fear of her torment, saying, Woe, woe, the great city, Babylon, the strong city! For in one hour is thy judgement come.**

What Moffatt calls 'this magnificent doom song' is modelled on the prophetic dirge over the city of Tyre (Ezek. 27). Kings (vv. 9, 10), merchants (vv. 11-17) and mariners (vv. 17-19) all mourn over the fall of Babylon. All cry, 'Woe', at the beginning of their lament and end with the words, 'in one hour' (vv. 10, 17, 19), thus marking the suddenness of the judgement 'with the monotony of a passing bell heard at intervals amid the strains of sad music' (Carpenter). Here the client kings of Rome wail over the fall of their seducer and protector ('the strong city'), because it has brought their own power and influence to a swift end.

v.11. **And the merchants of the earth weep and mourn over her, for no man buyeth their merchandise any more . . .**

The mourning of the merchants was also prompted by self-interest (Ezek. 27:28-36). Their prosperity had been founded upon Rome's insatiable appetite for the most expensive merchandise, and the sudden loss of this luxury market meant economic ruin for them.

vv.12, 13. **. . . merchandise of gold, and silver, and precious stone, and pearls, and fine linen, and purple, and silk, and scarlet: and all thyine wood, and every vessel of ivory, and every vessel made of most precious wood, and of brass, and iron, and marble; and cinnamon, and spice, and incense, and ointment, and frankin-**

cense, and wine, and oil, and fine flour, and wheat, and cattle, and sheep; and merchandise of horses and chariots and slaves; and souls of men.

This catalogue falls into six groups:

1. *Treasure:* gold, silver, precious stones and pearls;
2. *Expensive fabrics:* fine linen, purple, silk and scarlet;
3. *Materials used in furnishing:* citron wood, ivory, costly wood, bronze, iron and marble;
4. *Aromatic articles:* cinnamon, spice, incense, ointment and frankincense;
5. *Foods:* wine, oil, fine flour and wheat;
6. *Live stock:* cattle, sheep, horses, chariots and 'slaves, that is, human souls' (RSV).

The harlot's profligacy is demonstrated by the fact that the list thus concludes with the least valuable 'article'. 'The world of St John's day ministered in a thousand ways to the follies and vices of its Babylon, but the climax was reached in the sacrifice of human life which recruited the huge *familiae* of the rich, filled the *lupanaria* (brothels), and ministered to the brutal pleasures of the amphitheatre' (Swete).

v.14. **And the fruits which thy soul lusted after are gone from thee, and all things that were dainty and sumptuous are perished from thee, and men shall find them no more at all.**

In this verse Babylon herself is directly addressed. 'It is in harmony with the fervour of the whole chapter that the descriptive tone should for a moment give place to this apostrophe' (Carpenter). The fruits she lusted after are now gone for ever and the dainty luxuries and extravagant splendours have all disappeared.

vv.15-17a. **The merchants of these things, who were made rich by her, shall stand afar off for the fear of her torment, weeping and**

mourning; saying, Woe, woe, the great city, she that was arrayed
in fine linen and purple and scarlet, and decked with gold and
precious stone and pearl! For in one hour so great riches is made
desolate.

The merchants, like the kings, stand at a safe distance from the
city to bemoan their loss. Each group sees the fall of the city in
terms of its own interests. The kings lamented the fall of Rome's
power, whereas the merchants grieve over the sudden destruction
of her wealth.

vv.17b-19. **And every shipmaster, and every one that saileth any
whither, and mariners, and as many as gain their living by sea,
stood afar off, and cried out as they looked upon the smoke of
her burning, saying, What city is like the great city? And they
cast dust on their heads, and cried, weeping and mourning,
saying, Woe, woe, the great city, wherein all that had their
ships in the sea were made rich by reason of her costliness! For
in one hour is she made desolate.**

The third group who mourn the fall of the great city are the
sea-captains, passengers, sailors and those who earn their living
from the sea. They also view the disaster from a distance, but
they give more vivid expression to their sorrow by casting dust
upon their heads (Ezek. 27:30). However, their lament chiefly
concerns their own commercial loss, for they had profited from
the expensive goods in which Rome had so freely indulged.

v.20. **Rejoice over her, thou heaven, and ye saints, and ye apostles,
and ye prophets; for God hath judged your judgement on her.**

This further apostrophe (v. 14) is a call to the glorified church in
heaven to rejoice over the judgement of Babylon. It is not an
expression of vindictive delight in the suffering of the unrighteous, but 'a summons to all who have fought on the side of their

Lord to rejoice at the removal of one of the great obstacles to the manifestation of God's kingdom' (Carpenter). (See also comments on 6:9, 10.)

'**For God hath judged your judgement on her.**' Caird argues that this should be understood in the light of the law of malicious witness which required that the one who brought a false accusation should be repaid with the evil he intended for his brother (Deut. 19:16-19). Thus Babylon had brought malicious charges against Christians which resulted in their death, but she has been found guilty of perjury and now God has exacted the same penalty from her.

vv.21-23a. **And a strong angel took up a stone as it were a great millstone and cast it into the sea, saying, Thus with a mighty fall shall Babylon, the great city, be cast down, and shall be found no more at all. And the voice of harpers and minstrels and flute-players and trumpeters shall be heard no more at all in thee; and no craftsman, of whatsoever craft, shall be found any more at all in thee; and the voice of a mill shall be heard no more at all in thee; and the light of a lamp shall shine no more at all in thee; and the voice of the bridegroom and of the bride shall be heard no more at all in thee . . .**

In a symbolic act of judgement, a strong angel then took up a stone like a great millstone and hurled it into the sea, declaring that thus shall Babylon fall to rise no more (Jer. 51:63). The impressive repetition of the phrase 'no more at all' here rings out like a funeral knell over the dead city. No sound shall break the silence of the desolate place which was once throbbing with life. The strains of music are no longer heard in her; no craftsman pursues his trade; no grain is ground for bread; no lamp relieves her darkness and no marriages are celebrated in that house of death (Jer. 25:10).

vv.23b, 24. . . . . **for thy merchants were the princes of the earth;
for with thy sorcery were all the nations deceived. And in her
was found the blood of prophets and of saints, and of all that
have been slain upon the earth.**

The angel's proclamation concludes with three reasons for the
judgement of Babylon.
1.   Her merchant princes had acted as missionaries in corrupting the world with her false standards;
2.   She had also duped the nations with the sorcery of her
idolatries (Nahum 3:4; Rev. 17:2);
3.   In her was found the blood of all the saints (17:6).
    The last charge reveals the heinous nature of Babylon's guilt,
for, not content with rejecting the way of godliness herself, she
killed those who were faithfully following that path (cf. Matt.
23:35-39).

Revelation 19

The hymn of praise to God for judging the great harlot and avenging his martyred saints is followed by the marriage hymn of the Lamb (vv. 1-9). John is forbidden to worship the angel who showed him these things (v. 10). The Word of God appears at the head of his armies to destroy his enemies, and the beast and the false prophet are cast into the lake of fire (vv. 11-21).

vv.1, 2. After these things I heard as it were a great voice of a great multitude in heaven, saying, Hallelujah; Salvation, and glory, and power, belong to our God: for true and righteous are his judgements; for he hath judged the great harlot, her that corrupted the earth with her fornication, and he hath avenged the blood of her servants at her hand.

In this vision John hears a vast throng in heaven praising God for judging the great harlot and avenging the blood of his servants. The word 'Hallelujah' (= 'Praise ye Jehovah') introduces a number of Psalms (cf. Ps. 111:1; 112:1; 113:1; 146:1), but this is the only passage in the New Testament where it occurs (vv. 1, 3, 4, 6). Those familiar with Handel's *Messiah* cannot read this passage without being reminded of the great 'Hallelujah chorus', which consists of words taken from Revelation 19:6; 11:15; 19:16. The heavenly choir praises God as the author of that salvation which is effected by his glory and power. For by vindicating his servants and judging the harlot, he has again demonstrated that his judgements are true and righteous (15:3; 16:7). They are not capricious and arbitrary, but absolutely in accordance with the truth and justice of the case. She who had defiled the earth with her fornication and shed the blood of God's servants clearly deserved nothing but destruction!

v.3. **And a second time they say, Hallelujah. And her smoke goeth up for ever and ever.**

The image of Babylon's doom recalls the oracle against Edom (Isa. 34:10). 'The words are those of the Seer, who points to the unquenchable smoke rising as the accompaniment to the song and the proof of its truth' (Beckwith).

v.4. **And the four and twenty elders and the four living creatures fell down and worshipped God that sitteth on the throne, saying, Amen; Hallelujah.**

In their last appearance in the book of Revelation, the twenty-four elders and the four living beings confirm the praise of God's righteous judgements with this 'Amen' and add their own 'Hallelujah' (see comments on 4:4, 6, cf. Ps. 106:48).

v.5. **And a voice came forth from the throne, saying, Give praise to our God, all ye his servants, ye that fear him, the small and the great.**

'Our God' shows that the voice cannot be that of God or Christ; it must be that of one of the elders or living beings. The voice calls the whole church to join in the praise of God. (Ps. 113:1; 115:13). 'The small and the great' embraces all the redeemed, from the most insignificant saint to the greatest apostle (cf. 11:18).

vv.6-8. **And I heard as it were the voice of a great multitude, and** as the voice of many waters, and as the voice of mighty thunders, saying, Hallelujah: for the Lord our God, the Almighty, reigneth. Let us rejoice and be exceeding glad, and let us give the glory unto him: for the marriage of the Lamb is come, and his wife hath made herself ready. And it was given unto her that she should array herself in fine linen, bright and pure: for the fine linen is the righteous acts of the saints.

In response to this summons (v. 5), John heard the voice of a great multitude which was like the roar of many waters and great peals of thunder. The voice is not identified, but if the choir of verse 1 was angelic, then presumably this praise is offered by the innumerable company of the redeemed (cf. 7:9). The last hymn in the book strikes a new note of praise, for what the church celebrates is not the doom of Babylon, but its sequel in the setting up of the kingdom of God (cf. NEB: God . . . 'has entered on his reign!'). There is also rejoicing because the day of the Lamb's marriage has arrived. 'The marriage day of Christ and his church is the day of his second advent' (Moffatt). The most intimate of all relationships is a fit symbol of the union between Christ and his people, which will be perfected at his return (2 Cor. 11:2; Eph. 5:23-33). But though the marriage is here announced, the actual event is nowhere described, because even this metaphor cannot do justice to the reality it represents (1 John 3:2). The Lamb's wife has made herself ready by donning the divinely provided garment of fine linen. Her bridal dress is bright and pure, in marked contrast to the purple and scarlet garments of the great harlot (17:4). John explains that the fine linen stands for 'the righteous acts of the saints' (cf. Eph. 2:10). This is 'the sum of the saintly acts of the members of Christ, wrought in them by His Spirit . . . so corporately the whole Church is seen to be attired in the dazzling whiteness of their collective purity' (Swete).

v.9. **And he saith unto me, Write, Blessed are they that are bidden to the marriage supper of the Lamb. And he saith unto** me, These are true words of God.

The unnamed speaker is probably the interpreting angel of 17:1.
He commands John to write down the fourth beatitude in the
book, which concerns the blessedness of those who are called to
the marriage supper of the Lamb. This beatitude makes apparent
the fluidity of biblical metaphors, for the saints are not only
the bride, but are also the guests at the wedding! As the Spirit
endorses the beatitude spoken by a voice from heaven (14:13),
so the angel here confirms the truthfulness of these words of
God (Martin Rist).

v.10. **And I fell down before his feet to worship him. And he
saith unto me, See thou do it not: I am a fellow-servant with
thee and with thy brethren that hold the testimony of Jesus:
worship God: for the testimony of Jesus is the spirit of prophecy.**

John was so overwhelmed by this message that he fell at the feet
of the angel. But the angel rebuked him for offering to a fellow-
servant the worship that belongs to God, the giver of revelation
(v. 9; cf. comment on 1:2). According to the parallel passage
(22:9), it would appear that the brethren who hold the testimony
borne by Jesus are not simply believers but Christian prophets.
This helps to clarify the angel's explanation: 'For the testimony
of Jesus is the spirit of prophecy,' i.e. the testimony given by
Jesus is the word that the Spirit puts into the mouths of the
prophets. This is the special obligation resting upon them. 'They
have it, not as a secure possession, but as a task, i.e., in order that
they may pass it on, as John himself attests the witness of Jesus.
This is why they are prophets' (H. Strathmann, *TDNT,* Vol. IV,
p.501).

v.11. **And I saw the heaven opened; and behold, a white horse,
and he that sat thereon, called Faithful and True; and in righteousness he doth judge and make war.**

This section of the book reaches its climax in the vision of the conquering Messiah's return (vv. 11-21). As John sees heaven open, there appears a white horse of victory, whose rider is called Faithful and True. The title distinguishes Christ from the deceivers of mankind (vv. 19-21) and guarantees the reliability and truthfulness of his promises (cf. comment on 3:14). It is to fulfil those promises that he comes forth in righteousness to judge and make war on the beast and all his followers (Isa. 11:4; Ps. 96:13). 'The Christ who comes is both Judge and Warrior, and He judges first, for in the Divine order judgement precedes victory' (Swete).

v.12. **And his eyes are a flame of fire, and upon his head are many diadems; and he hath a name written, which no one knoweth but he himself.**

Nothing is hidden from the penetrating gaze of this Judge, whose eyes are like a flame of fire (1:14; 2:18). 'These *flame-like eyes* have been fixed upon the moving scenes of human life, and have been reading the hearts of men, and the true meaning of all events and actions' (Carpenter). Upon his head are many crowns of royalty which proclaim his universal kingship (v. 16; cf. 12:3; 13:1). In addition to the many titles which may be understood, he bears a name which is known to no one but himself, for 'only the Son of God can understand the mystery of His own Being' (Swete). (Matt. 11:27.)

v.13. **And he is arrayed in a garment sprinkled with blood: and his name is called The Word of God.**

As the symbol of his mission of vengeance (Isa. 63:1-6), the Rider wears a robe 'dipped in blood' (ASV margin). Christ's victory is so certain that he is here depicted as the Warrior whose garment is stained with the blood of his enemies before the battle is joined. He is fittingly called the Word of God because the punishment he inflicts upon them is the work of this all-powerful Word (cf. v. 15).

v.14. **And the armies which are in heaven followed him upon white horses, clothed in fine linen, white and pure.**

Mounted on white horses, the armies of heaven follow the conquering Messiah and share in his victory, while the purity of their dress shows that this is the triumph of righteousness. These are not the angels, but the overcomers of 17:14, the redeemed who follow the Lamb wherever he goes (14:4).

v.15. **And out of his mouth proceedeth a sharp sword, that with it he should smite the nations: and he shall rule them with a rod of iron: and he treadeth the winepress of the fierceness of the wrath of God, the Almighty.**

The only weapon which is used by Christ to judge the nations is the sharp sword which issues from his mouth (1:16). 'The sword is now wielded for but one work – the *word* that Christ spoke will judge men at the last day (John 12:48)' (Carpenter). The dreadful finality of this judgement is emphasized in three Old Testament figures: he smites the nations (Isa. 11:3, 4); he rules them with a rod of iron (Ps. 2:9); he treads the winepress of God's furious wrath (Isa. 63:1-6). Christ is the sole executor of that wrath. The armies who accompany him play no part in the judgement, but are simply witnesses of it.

v.16. **And he hath on his garment and on his thigh a name written, King of Kings, and Lord of Lords.**

'And on his thigh' explains where the name was written on his garment. It was emblazoned on that part of the garment which falls over the Rider's thigh, and was thus plainly visible to all.

So when Christ returns to judge the wicked, his absolute sovereignty will at last be acknowledged by all.

vv.17, 18. **And I saw an angel standing in the sun; and he cried with a loud voice, saying to all the birds that fly in mid-heaven, Come and be gathered together unto the great supper of God; that ye may eat the flesh of kings, and the flesh of captains, and the flesh of mighty men, and the flesh of horses and of them that sit thereon, and the flesh of all men, both free and bond, and small and great.**

In anticipation of Christ's triumph, an angel stands in the sun and calls the birds of prey in mid-air to come to the great supper that God has provided for them (Ezek. 39:17-20). This supper presents a grim contrast to the marriage supper of the Lamb (v. 9), for the feast consists of the flesh of God's enemies! The birds are invited to gorge themselves, not only on the flesh of kings and captains, but on that of men from every class. 'All classes — the great and small, the master and slave — are mentioned. Those who follow the world-power, and array themselves in hostility to the true King, belong not to one class, but may be found among all. The war is not between class and class, but between righteousness and unrighteousness, truth and falsehood, Christ and Belial' (Carpenter).

v.19. **And I saw the beast, and the kings of the earth, and their armies, gathered together to make war against him that sat upon the horse, and against his army.**

John sees the beast and his allies gathered together against the Lord's Anointed and his army (Ps. 2:2). The forces of evil willingly gather for the final conflict (16:14), but their plans are overruled by God and made to serve his ends. 'Those who take note of the tendencies of modern civilization will not find it impossible to conceive that a time may come when throughout Christendom the spirit of Antichrist will, with the support of

the State, make a final stand against a Christianity which is loyal
to the Person and teaching of Christ' (Swete).

vv. 20, 21. **And the beast was taken, and with him the false prophet
that wrought the signs in his sight, wherewith he deceived
them that had received the mark of the beast and them that
worshipped his image: they two were cast alive into the lake of
fire that burneth with brimstone: and the rest were killed with
the sword of him that sat upon the horse, even the sword which
came forth out of his mouth: and all the birds were filled with
their flesh.**

John gives no description of the battle, perhaps because the
mightiest army can do nothing against an omnipotent adversary.
Hence he simply records the outcome of the confrontation. The
beast and the false prophet were taken and cast into the lake of
fire (cf. 20:10); the rest were slain by the word of Christ (v. 15)
and their bodies devoured by the birds. 'Spiritual death is inflicted upon those who have proved themselves hostile to God.
The last sentence emphasizes the nature of the punishment by the
reference to the indignity offered to their bodies after death'
(Plummer).

Section 7

Christ's victory over Satan

Revelation 20

Satan is bound for a thousand years and the glorified saints reign with Christ for the same period (vv. 1-6). Satan is then released to gather the nations for the last battle. But the wicked are devoured by fire from heaven, and the devil is cast into the lake of fire (vv. 7-10). This is followed by the general resurrection and the last judgement (vv. 11-15).

v.1. **And I saw an angel coming down out of heaven, having the key of the abyss and a great chain in his hand.**

John sees an angel descend from heaven with the key of the abyss and a great chain in his hand. The angel does not act on his own initiative, but, like Michael, is authorized to put into effect the victory of Christ (see comment on 12:7). As the conqueror of Satan, Christ has the power to confine him to the abyss. But if this passage is regarded as a continuation of the previous chapter, then Christ refuses to exercise that power until the end of the age, a conclusion which is clearly at variance with the teaching of the entire New Testament!

vv.2, 3. **And he laid hold on the dragon, the old serpent, which is the Devil and Satan, and bound him for a thousand years, and cast him into the abyss, and shut it, and sealed it over him, that he should deceive the nations no more, until the thousand years should be finished: after this he must be loosed for a little time.**

John leaves us in no doubt of the identity of the one whom the angel binds and casts into the abyss (see comment on 12:9). Satan is thus bound for a thousand years so that he can no longer deceive the nations. If this follows the desolating judgement of chapter 19 in chronological sequence, it is rather surprising to find that there is anyone left to deceive! But the problem disappears when the thousand years are seen to be coextensive with the gospel age. This binding of Satan means that he cannot prevent the heralding of the gospel to all the nations (Lenski). It is Christ's victory over Satan that restrains him from deceiving the nations during the long day of grace (Matt. 12:26-29; 28:18-20; Luke 10:17-19; John 12:31, 32). But at the end of this period, Satan must be loosed for a little while to gather together the enemies of Christ for the last attack on his church (vv. 8, 9).

v.4. And I saw thrones, and they sat upon them, and judgement was given unto them: and I saw the souls of them that had been beheaded for the testimony of Jesus, and for the word of God, and such as worshipped not the beast, neither his image, and received not the mark upon their forehead and upon their hand; and they lived, and reigned with Christ a thousand years.

The scene now shifts from earth to heaven. 'Here is a vision of men from earth — not of men *on* it. That the expression ['the souls'] refers here to men in what is called the disembodied state, scarcely admits of question . . . The text indicates not that Christ came down to earth to live with them, but that they had soared upward to live and reign with Christ' (Clemance). John sees the believers who have died seated on thrones and sharing in the judgements of Christ (3:21). He then singles out for special mention the martyrs who, having refused to worship the beast, had suffered for the testimony of Jesus (13:15). These 'souls' lived and reigned with Christ 'a thousand years', i.e. throughout the gospel age (vv. 1-3). 'Those true to Christ during the comparatively brief period of persecution will reign with him for a long time. Again the very practical lesson is that it is worth dying to remain true to Christ' (Buis).

v.5. The rest of the dead lived not until the thousand years should be finished. This is the first resurrection.

What is true of the 'souls' in the previous verse does not pertain to 'the rest of the dead'. They do not 'live' in this period, as they are both physically and spiritually dead (though this does not mean that they cease to exist). And because they have not participated in the first resurrection, they are destined to suffer the second death (v. 6). 'The first resurrection is the rising of the saint at death to a higher life in Christ, which will be consummated at the general resurrection when the thousand years have expired' (Clemance).

v.6. Blessed and holy is he that hath part in the first resurrection: over these the second death hath no power; but they shall be priests of God and of Christ, and shall reign with him a thousand years.

This is the fifth beatitude in the book. Those who share in the first resurrection are pronounced blessed and holy. Not only does the second death have no power over them (v. 14), but they shall be priests of God and Christ, and they shall reign with him a thousand years (v. 4; 1:6; 5:10). 'They who are the Lord's rise twice, and die but once. They who are not the Lord's rise but once, and die twice' (Clemance).

vv. 7, 8. And when the thousand years are finished, Satan shall be loosed out of his prison, and shall come forth to deceive the nations which are in the four corners of the earth, Gog and Magog, to gather them together to the war: the number of whom is as the sand of the sea.

At the end of the gospel age, Satan will be released from his imprisonment and will go out to deceive the nations and gather them together for the final assault on God's people (v. 9). The passage emphasizes the crucial rôle of Satan at the end of the age, for his gathering of the nations for the last conflict leads to the dénouement of divine judgement. This is no new battle which unaccountably occurs at the end of an earthly millennium, but is in fact the same battle of Har-Magedon which has already been depicted three times in previous visions (cf. 16:12-16; 17:14-18; 19:11-21). The nations from the four corners of the earth are further identified as 'Gog and Magog' (Ezek. 38:2). As used by John, the term has no geographical significance, and has become the symbol of pagan opposition against God. This is in line with rabbinic thought, which equated Gog and Magog with the rebellious nations of Psalm 2. The final phrase points to an immense multitude.

v.9. **And they went up over the breadth of the earth, and compassed the camp of the saints about, and the beloved city: and fire came down out of heaven, and devoured them.**

The vast armies gathered by Satan advanced over the broad plain of the earth and encircled 'the camp of the saints' and 'the beloved city'. The people of God are here described under·the double symbolism of a camp and a city. The first image recalls the encampments of Israel in the wilderness (Exod. 14:19, 20; Num. 2), and the second distinguishes the community that willingly lives under the rule of God from the rebellious secular city. It is again made clear that no battle takes place, for fire descends from heaven and consumes this apparently invincible host (Ezek. 38:22; cf. 2 Thess. 1:7).

v.10. **And the devil that deceived them was cast into the lake of fire and brimstone, where are also the beast and the false prophet; and they shall be tormented day and night for ever and ever.**

The devil shares the same fate as the beast and the false prophet. This does not mean that they were cast into hell before Satan, but only that their punishment has already been described (19:20). 'They all go down together, Satan, the beast and the false prophet . . . In this lake of fire and brimstone all three are tormented for ever and ever (Matt. 25:46)' (Hendriksen).

v. 11. **And I saw a great white throne, and him that sat upon it, from whose face the earth and the heaven fled away; and there was found no place for them.**

The one whom John sees seated upon the great white throne is presumably God himself (5:1, 7, 13), but this should not be taken as excluding Christ from the judgement, since he also shares the throne with God (3:21; 22:1, 3). The majesty of the Judge was so awesome that even earth and heaven fled away, and no place was left for them. As Ladd rightly insists, the poetic imagery here conveys the profound theological truth that God's judgement must fall upon the creation, which was marred by man's sin (Rom. 8:19-22). Yet this judgement is not merely destructive, for the removal of the old order makes way for the new creation (2 Peter 3:13).

v. 12. **And I saw the dead, the great and the small, standing before the throne; and books were opened: and another book was opened, which is the book of life: and the dead were judged out of the things which were written in the books, according to their works.**

All the dead, both great and small, stand before the great white throne, and the books containing the record of their deeds are opened (Dan. 7:10). The judgements of the last assize are not arbitrary, but are in perfect accord with the evidence thus presented (2:23; 22:12; Rom. 2:6). Then another book is opened to reveal the names of those elected to eternal life (3:5; 13:8;

17:8; 21:27). The principle of judgement according to works cannot disclose any disagreement between the testimony of the books and the book of life. 'Judgement according to works does not contravene salvation by grace. Salvation is by grace through faith. But the faith that is saving bears fruit in good works, and faith without works is dead. Good works are therefore the index to a state of salvation' (John Murray, *Collected Writings: 2*, p.416).

v.13. **And the sea gave up the dead that were in it; and death and Hades gave up the dead that were in them: and they were judged every man according to their works.**

The sea is specially mentioned to show that 'the accidents of death will not prevent any of the dead from appearing before the Judge' (Swete). In the ancient world death by drowning was considered to be a desolate fate, as it meant that the body could not be buried properly, and some Jews believed that this made resurrection impossible (Bruce). The universal extent of the resurrection is emphasized by the statement that death and Hades gave up the dead that were in them (cf. 1:18). Not only are all the dead included in the judgement, but it is again affirmed that all are judged according to their works (v. 12).

vv.14, 15. **And death and Hades were cast into the lake of fire. This is the second death, even the lake of fire. And if any was not found written in the book of life, he was cast into the lake of fire.**

This bold personification signifies the end of the intermediate state. As the realm of the dead, Hades receives souls after death, and then delivers them up again at the resurrection. The resurrection marks its end, and it is replaced by hell as the final place of punishment (J. Jeremias, *TDNT*, Vol. I, p.148). Anyone whose name was not found written in the book of life was cast into the lake of fire, which is the second death (21:8). As in Matthew 25:40-46, the qualification for the second death is a negative one, because the 'negation of eternal life is eternal death' (Swete).

Revelation 21

In a vision of a new heaven and earth, John sees the new Jeru-salem coming down from heaven (vv. 1, 2). The blessedness of God's people is described and the judgement of the wicked con-firmed (vv. 3-8). The chapter concludes with a glowing account of the splendours of the new Jerusalem (vv. 9-27).

v.1. **And I saw a new heaven and a new earth: for the first heaven and the first earth are passed away; and the sea is no more.**

The judgement which removed the old order makes way for a new heaven and a new earth (cf. 20:11; Isa. 65:17). Here 'new' (*kainos*) does not mean new in time, but new in quality. The new order does not evolve from the historical process, but is entirely due to the creative interposition of God. There is no room in the new earth for the sea, as it is the symbol of separation, wicked-ness and restless rebellion (13:1; Ps. 65:7; 93:3; Isa. 57:20). The sea has disappeared, because 'it is associated with ideas which are at variance with the character of the New Creation' (Swete).

v.2. **And I saw the holy city, new Jerusalem, coming down out of heaven from God, made ready as a bride adorned for her husband.**

John depicts the bliss of the perfected community under the dual image of a city and a bride. He sees the holy city, new

Jerusalem (cf. v. 1), coming down out of heaven from God, prepared as a bride adorned for her husband (19:7). The continuity of God's redemptive purpose is indicated by the name of the city, new *Jerusalem,* which stands for the whole church of God, including the saints of both dispensations. The city descends *from* heaven because the church is God's creation; it descends *to* earth for that is where the glorified saints will enjoy uninterrupted fellowship with God throughout eternity (v. 3).

v.3. And I heard a great voice out of the throne saying, Behold, the tabernacle of God is with men, and he shall dwell with them, and they shall be his peoples, and God himself shall be with them, and be their God ...

John then heard a great voice from the throne announcing the ultimate fulfilment of the Old Testament promise (Lev. 26:11, 12; Ezek. 37:27; Zech. 8:8). 'Behold' arrests the attention and marks the wonder of the permanent tabernacling of God with men. The original promise to Israel is here expanded to include men of all nations who now constitute 'his peoples' (7:9). The assurance that God will be with them and be their God is an obvious echo of the Immanuel prophecy (Isa. 7:14).

v.4. . . . and he shall wipe away every tear from their eyes; and death shall be no more; neither shall there be mourning, nor crying, nor pain, any more: the first things are passed away.

The blessedness of eternal fellowship with God means that the first things which belonged to the old order have passed away. Gone for ever is that grim harvest of sin: sorrow, suffering and death. God will graciously console his people by wiping away every tear from their eyes (Isa. 25:8). 'So many descriptions of eternal blessedness are either figurative or couched in negation because the realities are inconceivable to us in our present state' (Lenski).

v.5. **And he that sitteth on the throne said, Behold, I make all things new. And he saith, Write: for these words are faithful and true.**

Apart from 1:8, this paragraph is the only place in Revelation where God is definitely represented as the speaker (vv. 5-8; cf. 16:1, 17). It is from the throne that the sovereign God declares that he is making all things new. There is nothing that can frustrate the fulfilment of his creative purpose and therefore the regeneration which is rooted in Christ's redemptive achievement shall be consummated in the cosmic renewal of all things (2 Cor. 5:17). God commands John to write down this message to the churches, because the revelation is trustworthy and true (19:9; 22:6).

v.6. **And he said unto me, They are come to pass. I am the Alpha and the Omega, the beginning and the end. I will give unto him that is athirst of the fountain of the water of life freely.**

God here proclaims that these things have come to pass, because the future blessedness of the saints is so secure that it can be regarded as already accomplished. For he who is the Alpha and Omega determines both the beginning and the end according to the counsel of his own will (1:8; Eph. 1:11). To the one who thirsts for him, God offers to give of the fountain of the water of life freely (22:17; Ps. 42:1, 2; 63:1; Isa. 55:1, 2; Matt. 5:6).

v.7. **He that overcometh shall inherit these things; and I will be his God, and he shall be my son.**

As in the letters to the seven churches, it is the victor in the present spiritual conflict who shall inherit all the blessings of the new creation (2:7, 11, 17, 26; 3:5, 12, 21). 'I will be his God, and he shall be my son' further defines the promise of the previous verse; 'the thirst for God will be satisfied in the relation of perfect sonship with God' (Beckwith). It is significant that the Messianic prophecy of 2 Samuel 7:14 could only be applied to the Christian when the word 'father' was replaced by 'God', for God is uniquely the Father of Christ and believers are God's sons only by the adoption of grace.

v.8. **But for the fearful, and unbelieving, and abominable, and murderers, and fornicators, and sorcerers, and idolaters, and all liars, their part shall be in the lake that burneth with fire and brimstone; which is the second death.**

In contrast to the assurance given to the overcomer, God warns that the lot of the wicked shall be in the lake of fire, which is the second death (20:14, 15). Those who exclude themselves from the holy city are characterized by eight epithets (cf. 22:15). Perhaps only the first two relate to apostates, and the rest apply to pagans in general. 'The cowardly' and 'the faithless' are those who have denied the faith under the pressure of persecution. 'Abominable' describes those who shared in the impurities of the harlot (17:4, 5). In this context 'murderers' possibly refers to the persecutors who killed the martyrs (13:15). 'Fornicators', 'sorcerers' and 'idolaters' are common descriptions of the heathen, while 'liars' includes all the lovers and inventors of falsehoods (2:2; 3:9; 14:5; 21:27; 22:15). These all have their place in the lake of fire, because their 'moral affinities are with evil . . . Character determines environment, and character is destiny' (R. A. Finlayson, *God's Light on Man's Destiny,* p.66).

v.9. **And there came one of the seven angels who had the seven bowls, who were laden with the seven last plagues; and he spake with me, saying, Come hither, I will show thee the bride, the wife of the Lamb.**

One of the angels with the seven bowls, presumably the angel who had shown John the great harlot (17:1), now comes to show him the bride, the wife of the Lamb (v. 2). The use of the same angel to introduce both visions thus presents a striking contrast between the doom of the harlot city and the glory of the holy city.

v.10. **And he carried me away in the Spirit to a mountain great and high, and showed me the holy city Jerusalem, coming down out of heaven from God . . .**

The angel carried John away in the Spirit to a high mountain, and there showed him 'the holy city' Jerusalem descending from God out of heaven (Ezek. 40:2). What is stressed here is not the newness of Jerusalem (v. 2), but her distinctive character as the holy city. This shows that the purpose of the vision is not so much predictive as pastoral, for the holiness of the glorified church provides a great incentive for holy living in the present age.

v.11. **. . . having the glory of God: her light was like unto a stone most precious, as it were a jasper stone, clear as crystal . . .**

The most important feature of the holy city is mentioned first. John saw that it shone with the glory of God, 'and its brilliance was like that of a very precious jewel, like a jasper, clear as crystal' (NIV, cf. 4:3). And because the city thus rejoiced in the light of God's own presence, it needed no other source of illumination (21:23).

vv.12, 13. **. . . having a wall great and high; having twelve gates, and at the gates twelve angels; and names written thereon, which are the names of the twelve tribes of the children of Israel: on the east were three gates; and on the north three gates; and on the south three gates; and on the west three gates.**

The city is square, and is surrounded by a great wall with three gates on each side, on which are inscribed the names of the twelve tribes of Israel (Ezek. 48:30-34). In the new Jerusalem each tribe of the whole Israel of God (see comment on 7:4) 'is assured of its right of equal approach into the place of God's presence' (Beckwith). To allow easy access for the elect the gates of the city are never shut (v. 25), but to protect its purity each gate has its guardian angel (Isa. 62:6; Rev. 22:15).

v.14. **And the wall of the city had twelve foundations, and on them twelve names of the twelve apostles of the Lamb.**

The wall of the city rests on twelve foundations, upon which are inscribed the names of the twelve apostles of the Lamb. The thought is similar to that of Ephesians 2:20. The church is founded upon the apostolic testimony to Christ. Since the apostolate as a whole is in view, there can be 'no question as to individual names of apostles, e.g. whether St Matthias or St Paul is the twelfth' (Plummer).

v.15. **And he that spake with me had for a measure a golden reed to measure the city, and the gates thereof, and the wall thereof.**

The angel had a golden reed to measure the city, so that John might realize its vast size and admire its perfect symmetry (Ezek. 40:3).

vv.16, 17. **And the city lieth foursquare, and the length thereof is as great as the breadth: and he measured the city with the reed, twelve thousand furlongs: the length and the breadth and the height thereof are equal. And he measured the wall thereof, a hundred and forty and four cubits, according to the measure of a man, that is, of an angel.**

The city is in the shape of a perfect cube, and thus corresponds to the Holy of Holies in the temple (1 Kings 6:20). The high priest could only enter the holy place once a year, but free access to God is the constant privilege of all the inhabitants of this city. Although John tells us that the angel was using the human system of measurements, the enormous dimensions of the city are clearly symbolic, and the attempts to reduce them to a mathematical statement are quite futile (Vincent). No light is thrown on the passage by observing that the city extends for 1500 miles in each direction and that its walls are 216 feet thick! The numbers are again in multiples of twelve, and simply indicate that there will be plenty of room in the city for all the people of God.

v. 18. **And the building of the wall thereof was jasper: and the city was pure gold, like unto pure glass.**

The wall of the city was built of jasper, which shows that even its boundaries were suffused with the glory of God (v. 11). The city itself was built of gold so pure that it was like clear glass. This image perhaps points to the purity of the glorified church (Eph. 5:27).

vv. 19, 20. **The foundations of the wall of the city were adorned with all manner of precious stones. The first foundation was jasper; the second, sapphire; the third, chalcedony; the fourth, emerald; the fifth, sardonyx; the sixth, sardius; the seventh, chrysolite; the eighth, beryl; the ninth, topaz; the tenth, chrysoprase; the eleventh, jacinth; the twelfth, amethyst.**

The glory of the city is further enhanced by the precious stones which adorn the foundations of the wall (Isa. 54:11, 12). These gems recall the jewelled breastplate of the high priest, on which were engraved the names of the twelve tribes of Israel (Exod. 28:15-21). Most of the stones are the same in both lists, and 'their function here is to express the priestly character of Christ and his church as the foundation of the renewed world' (John Sweet).

v.21. And the twelve gates were twelve pearls; each one of the several gates was of one pearl: and the street of the city was pure gold, as it were transparent glass.

Each of the twelve gates of the city consisted of a single pearl. Although we cannot imagine pearls of such a size, the image suggests the transcendent worth of the kingdom, and brings to mind the parable of the merchant who sold all to gain the pearl of greatest price (Matt. 13:45, 46). The main street of the city was made of pure gold which looked like transparent glass. The royal dignity of walking upon gold belongs to those who are joint-heirs with Christ.

v.22. And I saw no temple therein: for the Lord God the Almighty, and the Lamb, are the temple thereof.

In sharp contrast to Ezekiel's vision of the restored temple (Ezek. 40-46), John sees that there is no temple in the new Jerusalem, for the city itself is now the Holy of Holies (see comment on v. 16). 'No temple building is needed, for the presence of God and the Lamb makes every place where they are a sanctuary, and the whole new Jerusalem is filled with their presence' (Beckwith).

v.23. And the city hath no need of the sun, neither of the moon, to shine upon it: for the glory of God did lighten it, and the lamp thereof is the Lamb.

As the divine Presence removes the need for any material temple in the city (v. 22), so it needs no created light, since the same Presence illuminates it unceasingly (Isa. 60:19, 20). Another indirect proof of the deity of Christ is provided by this further linking together of God and the Lamb (cf. 22:3).

v.24. **And the nations shall walk amidst the light thereof: and the kings of the earth bring their glory into it.**

Here the unversal diffusion of the knowledge of God in the eternal order is expressed in the language of Old Testament prophecy. Isaiah spoke of the day when the brightness of God's presence in Jerusalem would attract the homage of Gentile nations and kings (Isa. 60:1-3). It is appropriate for John to apply this prophecy to the eternal state, because the redeemed are drawn from all the nations of the earth (7:9). As it appears that these peoples will retain their national identity, the saints of each nation will have a distinctive contribution to make to the glory of God (cf. v. 26).

v.25. **And the gates thereof shall in no wise be shut by day (for there shall be no night there)** . . .

This is taken from Isaiah 60:11, but because Isaiah says the gates 'shall not be shut day *nor night*', John adds his parenthetical remark to explain this omission. 'In peace by day, the city gates will be open; nor can there be night when God the Almighty is the Sun' (Carpenter).

v.26. . . . **and they shall bring the glory and the honour of the nations into it** . . .

This further allusion to Isaiah 60:11 reaffirms the thought of verse 24 (see comment there).

v.27. . . . **and there shall in no wise enter into it anything unclean,**

or he that maketh an abomination and a lie: but only they that are written in the Lamb's book of life.

The unclean shall not enter the holy city, but only those whose names are written in the Lamb's book of life (20:15). John warns his readers that no one who now indulges in the impurities of Babylon shall gain access to the new Jerusalem (22:15). For the freedom of that city belongs to those who have made their calling and election sure by the obedience of faith (22:14). 'The Bible does not teach universalism. Here is great blessedness for God's people, but those who remain in their sin are excluded' (Buis).

Revelation 22

After the vision of the river and tree of life, the blessedness of God's servants is described (vv. 1-7). John is forbidden by the angel to worship him and is commanded to seal up the prophecy (vv. 8-11). The promise of Christ's coming is followed by the response of the Spirit and the church (vv. 12-17). John adds a solemn warning against tampering with the teaching of the book and concludes with the benediction (vv. 18-21).

vv.1, 2a. **And he showed me a river of water of life, bright as crystal, proceeding out of the throne of God and of the Lamb, in the midst of the street thereof.**

The first five verses of this chapter conclude John's vision of the new Jerusalem and provide a brief but glorious description of what life is like in the city. Eternal life in all its fulness is symbolized by the river of the water of life, which flows out from the throne through the midst of the city (Ps. 46:4). The image recalls the river of Eden (Gen. 2:10) and the river that flowed from the temple in Ezekiel's vision (Ezek. 47:1-12). But as there is no temple in the holy city, the source of this river is the throne of God and of the Lamb, who are thus regarded as the joint source of the blessing.

v.2b. **And on this side of the river and on that was the tree of life, bearing twelve manner of fruits, yielding its fruit every**

month: and the leaves of the tree were for the healing of the nations.

Here the singular 'tree' is used collectively, for each side of the river was lined with these trees. They produced twelve kinds of fruit every month, and their leaves 'were for the healing of the nations' (Ezek. 47:12). This does not mean that there is any disease which needs healing in the new Jerusalem. The expression simply contrasts the suffering of the present life with the complete absence of all ills in the next. Hence 'the tree of life' is another symbol of eternal life (2:7; 22:14). It brings to mind the tree in Eden from which man was barred after he had sinned (Gen. 2:9; 3:22). 'The consummation of God's dealings with creation and man thus takes up and transcends what was given in Paradise' (K. Rengstorf, *TDNT,* Vol. VI, p.604).

v.3. **And there shall be no curse any more: and the throne of God and of the Lamb shall be therein: and his servants shall serve him . . .**

In contrast to the present evil age, there shall be no more curse in the new Jerusalem, because the rule of God and the Lamb banishes all sin (Gen. 3:17; Zech. 14:11). Their unity is such that they share the same throne and the same glory, and their servants are said to serve '*him*' (John 10:30). 'To the final revelation of God there corresponds a perfected service; where the Throne is always in sight the service must be perpetual' (Swete). (Cf. 7:15.)

v.4. **. . . and they shall see his face; and his name shall be on their foreheads.**

What was denied to Moses will be the ultimate privilege of all God's people (Exod. 33:20). 'To see God is the reward of purity, and conversely the sight of God in Christ will perfect the process of purification (Matt. 5:8; 1 John 3:2)' (Swete). As a mark

of ownership, they will bear on their foreheads the name of God
(3:12). Since each epoch of God's self-revelation to man was
associated with some new name of God, it is not surprising that
the future age will be marked by a further disclosure of the divine
glory (T. F. Glasson).

v.5. **And there shall be night no more; and they need no light of
lamp, neither light of sun; for the Lord God shall give them
light: and they shall reign for ever and ever.**

Darkness is utterly banished from the holy city, where there is no
night and no need of lamp or sun, for its inhabitants will rejoice
in the radiance of the Lord God (21:23). And they shall reign
for ever and ever (3:21). With this final promise of the unending
bliss of the redeemed the visions of the Apocalypse reach a
fitting conclusion.

v.6. **And he said unto me, These words are faithful and true:
and the Lord, the God of the spirits of the prophets, sent his
angel to show unto his servants the things which must shortly
come to pass.**

The epilogue to the whole book begins with the angel's guarantee
of its veracity. He tells John that these words are trustworthy
and true (21:5) for they come from the Lord, who sent his
angel to show his servants the things that must shortly come
to pass (see comment on 1:1). The remarkable expression, 'the
God of the spirits of the prophets', is clarified by 19:10. It means
that God illuminates the spirits of the prophets by the inspiration
of the Holy Spirit; 'they are the natural faculties of the Prophets,
raised and quickened by the Holy Spirit' (Swete).

v.7. **And behold, I come quickly. Blessed is he that keepeth the
words of the prophecy of this book.**

The angel here quotes the words of Christ and does so again in verse 12. As the nearness of the Lord's advent should promote watchfulness, this announcement is appropriately followed by the sixth beatitude in the book, which pronounces a blessing upon the obedient. 'It is not in reading, or wondering, or talking, but in keeping, that the blessing comes. He that loves Christ will keep His commandments (John 14:15), even as Christ loved His Father and kept His commandments (John 15:10)' (Carpenter).

vv.8, 9. **And I John am he that heard and saw these things. And when I heard and saw, I fell down to worship before the feet of the angel that showed me these things. And he saith unto me, See thou do it not: I am a fellow-servant with thee and with thy brethren the prophets, and with them that keep the words of this book: worship God.**

John now vouches for the authenticity of the revelation he has received, and confesses that he was so overcome by the divine authority of the message that he fell at the feet of the angel through whom it was mediated (19:10). But the angel forbids the homage and directs him to worship God, because he is only a fellow-servant with John and his brethren the prophets, and with all the faithful who keep the words of the book.

v.10. **And he saith unto me, Seal not up the words of the prophecy of this book; for the time is at hand.**

Daniel was told to seal up the words of the book (Dan. 12:4, 9), but John must publish the prophecy for the encouragement of the churches. In Daniel's case the end was far off, but now the time is at hand. Such is the difference between the prophecy of the old and the new dispensation. The first belonged to the preliminary state; the other to the final fulfilment. So however 'long the gospel age may have lasted, or may yet continue, *it is the last time* (1 John 2:18)' (Carpenter).

v.11. **He that is unrighteous, let him do unrighteousness still: and he that is filthy, let him be made filthy still: and he that is righteous, let him do righteousness still: and he that is holy, let him be made holy still.**

The apparent determinism of the verse in fact conceals a solemn warning and an implicit appeal to the readers (Dan. 12:10). There is obvious irony in commanding the wicked to continue in their evil ways. But the intention is surely to show that as character determines destiny, so the time will soon come when change is no longer possible. Although the exhortation to the righteous presents no problem, it is equally relevant since only those who endure to the end shall be saved (Matt. 10:22).

vv.12, 13. **Behold, I come quickly; and my reward is with me, to render to each man according as his work is. I am the Alpha and the Omega, the first and the last, the beginning and the end.**

Once more the angel quotes the words of Christ (v. 7). He will come quickly to reward the righteous and the wicked by rendering 'to each man according as his work is' (see comment on 20:12). The total life of each man will be 'his work': 'the public evidence of what is in his heart, either faith or unbelief' (Lenski). The titles claimed by God (1:8; 21:6) also belong to Christ (1:17; 2:8), and they here give solemn assurance that he has the divine authority to judge all men. It is because God and the Lamb share the same throne (v. 1) that the judgement-seat of Christ is also the judgement-seat of God (Rom. 14:10; 2 Cor. 5:10).

v.14. **Blessed are they that wash their robes, that they may have the right to come to the tree of life, and may enter in by the gates into the city.**

The evangelical tone of the last beatitude in the book is unmistakable. The blessing is pronounced upon those who wash their robes, for only they have the right to the tree of life, and may enter in triumph through the gates of the city (see comment on v. 2b). This washing of their robes in the blood of the Lamb must continue throughout their earthly pilgrimage, whereas the washing is regarded as past when the glorified saints are in view (cf. 7:14). The right to eternal life rests entirely upon washing in the blood of Christ the garments soiled by sin.

> Dear dying Lamb, Thy precious blood
> Shall never lose its power,
> Till all the ransomed church of God
> Be saved to sin no more.
> *William Cowper*

v. 15. **Without are the dogs, and the sorcerers, and the fornicators, and the murderers, and the idolaters, and every one that loveth and maketh a lie.**

This verse does not mean that the wicked are just outside the holy city, but rather emphasizes their eternal exclusion from it. Five of the six types of evildoers mentioned also appear in 21:8, but the term 'dogs' significantly heads the list. The wild scavenging dogs which roamed about eastern cities were a fit symbol of the unclean and the impure. 'All liars' (21:8) is here expanded to 'every one that loveth and maketh a lie'. 'He who loves falsehood is in his nature akin to it, and has through his love of it proved his affinity to Satan, who is *the father of it* (John 8:44)' (Swete).

v. 16. **I Jesus have sent mine angel to testify unto you these things for the churches. I am the root and the offspring of David, the bright, the morning star.**

The emphatic 'I Jesus' shows that this is the direct utterance of Christ. He has sent his angel 'to testify unto you these things for the churches'. As 'you' is plural, it would seem that the seven churches are addressed. If so 'the churches' would then refer to the churches outside Asia. Jesus presents himself as 'the root and offspring of David' because he is the fulfilment of the Messianic promise (Isa. 11:1; cf. Rev. 5:5). He is also 'the bright, the morning star' who heralds the dawn of everlasting day (Num. 24:17; 2 Peter 1:19).

v.17. **And the Spirit and the bride say, Come. And he that heareth, let him say, Come. And he that is athirst, let him come: he that will, let him take the water of life freely.**

'Come' is the ardent response of the Holy Spirit and the church to the words of the Lord, and every man who listens to the reading of the book is bidden to join in this prayer for the Lord's return. Finally, any outsider who is thirsty is urged to come and take the water of life freely (21:6). Although the supply is gratuitous, 'take' suggests that 'the responsibility of accepting and using it rests with the individual' (Swete).

vv.18, 19. **I testify unto every man that heareth the words of the prophecy of this book, If any man shall add unto them, God shall add unto him the plagues which are written in this book: and if any man shall take away from the words of the book of this prophecy, God shall take away his part from the tree of life, and out of the holy city, which are written in this book.**

John issues a severe warning against tampering with the message of the book (Deut. 4:2; 12:32). If any man adds words of his own God shall add to him the plagues threatened in it, and if any man takes away any words God shall take away his part from the tree of life and the holy city. By this wilful distortion of God's Word he would forfeit 'his share' of eternal life, i.e. he would lose what he seemed to have by profession, though as such an act would prove, not by possession!

v.20. **He who testifieth these things saith, Yea: I come quickly. Amen: come, Lord Jesus.**

The book concludes with Christ's promise to come quickly, and the response of the church is expressed by John: 'Come, Lord Jesus'. This expression is the equivalent of the Aramaic saying, *Maranatha* (1 Cor. 16:22). 'It is the cry of the waiting and longing community for His coming again in glory — a cry which is made to the Lord of the community with particular force and fervour at the Lord's Supper ("Lord, come")' (K. G. Kuhn, *TDNT*, Vol. IV, p.472).

v.21. **The grace of the Lord Jesus be with the saints. Amen.**

Since the opening of the book has the form of an epistle (1:4), it ends appropriately with a benediction. John prays that the grace of the Lord Jesus may be with the saints of Asia who have heard the prophecy read to them in church.

Soli Deo Gloria

Bibliography

Arndt, W. F., and Gingrich, F. W., *A Greek-English Lexicon of the New Testament,* (University of Chicago Press, 1957).

Ashcraft, Morris, *Revelation,* (Broadman Bible Commentary, 1972).

Banks, Robert (ed.), *Reconciliation and Hope,* (Eerdmans, 1974).

Beasley-Murray, G. R., *The Book of Revelation,* (Oliphants, 1974).

Beckwith, Isbon T., *The Apocalypse of John,* (Baker, 1967).

Berkhof, L., *Systematic Theology,* (Banner of Truth, 1959).

Bowman, John Wick, 'The Revelation of John: Its Dramatic Structure and Message' (from *Interpretation,* October 1955).

Bruce, F. F., *Revelation* – A Bible Commentary for Today, (Pickering & Inglis, 1979).

Buis, Harry, *The Book of Revelation* – A Simplified Commentary, (Presbyterian & Reformed, 1974).

Buis, Harry, *The Doctrine of Eternal Punishment,* (Presbyterian & Reformed, 1957).

Caird, G. B., *The Revelation of St John the Divine,* (A. & C. Black, 1966).

Carpenter, W. Boyd, *The Revelation of St John* – Bible Commentary for English Readers, ed. C. J. Ellicott, Vol. VIII) (Cassell)

Charles, R. H., *The Revelation of St John,* (ICC), (T. & T. Clark, 1975).

Finlayson, R. A., *God's Light on Man's Destiny,* (Knox Press, Edinburgh).

Glasson, T. F., *The Revelation of John,* (CBC), (CUP, 1965).

Grier, W. J., *The Momentous Event,* (Banner of Truth, 1970).

Guthrie, Donald, *New Testament Introduction*, (Tyndale, 1970).

Harrison, Everett F., (ed.,) *Baker's Dictionary of Theology*, (Baker, 1960).

Hendriksen, William, *More than Conquerors*, (Tyndale, 1962).

Hoekema, Anthony A., *The Bible and the Future*, (Eerdmans, 1979).

Hort, F. J. A., *Expository and Exegetical Studies*, (Klock & Klock, 1980).

Hughes, P. E., *Interpreting Prophecy*, (Eerdmans, 1976).

Johnson, Alan F., *Revelation*, (EBC), (Zondervan, 1981).

Jones, R. Bradley, *What, Where, and When is the Millennium?*, (Baker, 1975).

Kiddle, Martin, *The Revelation of St John*, (MNTC), (Hodder & Stoughton, 1940).

Kittel, G., (ed.,) *Theological Dictionary of the New Testament*, trans. Geoffrey Bromiley, (Eerdmans, 1964 – 76).

Ladd, George Eldon, *A Commentary on the Revelation of John*, (Eerdmans, 1972).

Lenski, R. C. H., *The Interpretation of St John's Revelation*, (Augsburg, 1943).

McKelvey, R. J., *The New Temple*, (OUP, 1969).

Metzger, Bruce M., *A Textual Commentary on the Greek New Testament*, (UBS, 1971).

Moffatt, James, *Revelation*, (EGT), (Eerdmans, 1974).

Morris, Leon, *Apocalyptic*, (IVP, 1972).

Morris, Leon, *Revelation*, (TNTC), (Tyndale, 1969).

Mounce, Robert H., *The Book of Revelation*, (NICNT), (Eerdmans, 1977).

Murray, George L., *Millennial Studies*, (Baker, 1977).

Murray, John, *Collected Writings 2: Systematic Theology*, (Banner of Truth, 1977).

Plummer, A., and Clemance, C., *Revelation*, (Pulpit Commentary), (Kegan Paul, 1890).

Preston, R. H., and Hanson, A. T., *Revelation of Saint John the Divine*, (TBC), (SCM, 1968).

Ramsay, W. M., *The Letters to the Seven Churches of Asia*, (James, 1978).

Robertson, A. T., *Word Pictures in the New Testament*, Vol. VI, (Broadman Press, 1931).

Robbins, Ray Frank, *The Revelation of Jesus Christ*, (Broadman Press, 1975).

Rist, Martin, *The Revelation of St John the Divine,* (IB), (Abingdon, 1957).

Shedd, W. G. T., *The Doctrine of Endless Punishment,* (Klock & Klock, 1980).

Shedd, W. G. T., *Dogmatic Theology,* (Klock & Klock, 1979).

Shedd, W. G. T., *Sermons to the Spiritual Man,* (Banner of Truth 1972).

Skilton, John H., (ed.,) *The Law and the Prophets,* (Presbyterian & Reformed, 1974).

Stonehouse, N. B., *Paul before the Areopagus and other New Testament Studies,* (Tyndale, 1957).

Sweet, John, *Revelation,* (SCM Pelican), (SCM, 1979).

Swete, H. B., *The Apocalypse of St John,* (Macmillan, 1909).

Trench, R. C., *The Epistles to the Seven Churches in Asia,* (Macmillan, 1867).

Vincent, Marvin R., *Word Studies in the New Testament,* (MacDonald).

Vos, Geerhardus, *Redemptive History and Biblical Interpretation,* (Presbyterian & Reformed, 1980).

Warfield, B. B., *The Works of Benjamin B. Warfield: II Biblical Doctrines,* (Baker, 1981).

Warfield, B. B., *Selected Shorter Writings of Benjamin B. Warfield: II,* ed. John E. Meeter, (Presbyterian & Reformed, 1973).

Yamauchi, Edwin, *The Archaeology of New Testament Cities in Western Asia Minor,* (Pickering & Inglis, 1980).

Zorn, Raymond O., *Church and Kingdom,* (Presbyterian & Reformed, 1962).